# Dogs of the North

Volume 14, Number 1 / 1987
ALASKA GEOGRAPHIC®

# The Alaska Geographic Society

*To teach many more to better know and use our natural resources*

**Editor:** Penny Rennick
**Associate Editor:** Kathy Doogan
**Editorial Assistant:** Laurie Thompson
**Designer:** Sandra Harner

ALASKA GEOGRAPHIC®, ISSN 0361-1353, is published quarterly by The Alaska Geographic Society, Anchorage, Alaska 99509-3370. Second-class postage paid in Edmonds, Washington 98020-3588. Printed in U.S.A. Copyright© 1987 by The Alaska Geographic Society. All rights reserved. Registered trademark; Alaska Geographic, ISSN 0361-1353; Key title Alaska Geographic.

THE ALASKA GEOGRAPHIC SOCIETY is a nonprofit organization exploring new frontiers of knowledge across the lands of the polar rim, learning how other men and other countries live in their Norths, putting the geography book back in the classroom, exploring new methods of teaching and learning — sharing in the excitement of discovery in man's wonderful new world north of 51°16′.

MEMBERS OF THE SOCIETY RECEIVE *Alaska Geographic*®, a quality magazine which devotes each quarterly issue to monographic in-depth coverage of a northern geographic region or resource-oriented subject.

**THE COVER:** *Joe Redington Sr. takes his dogs for a training run. Redington likes to begin with slow, five-mile training runs, gradually increasing the mileage to build up the dogs' muscles* (J. Schultz)

**PREVIOUS PAGE:** *Niki, a purebred Samoyed owned by John Madden of Anchorage, pauses to enjoy a spectacular view during one of their frequent outings.* (John Madden)

**OPPOSITE:** *Its coat fluffed against the cold, a malemute tries to find some warmth in the mid-winter sun.* (J. Schultz)

MEMBERSHIP DUES in The Alaska Geographic Society are $30 per year; $34 to non-U.S. addresses. (Eighty percent of each year's dues is for a one-year subscription to *Alaska Geographic*®.) Order from The Alaska Geographic Society, Box 93370, Anchorage, Alaska 99509-3370; (907) 258-2515.

MATERIAL SOUGHT: The editors of *Alaska Geographic*® seek a wide variety of informative material on the lands north of 51°16′ on geographic subjects — anything to do with resources and their uses (with heavy emphasis on quality color photography) — from Alaska, northern Canada, Siberia, Japan — all geographic areas that have a relationship to Alaska in a physical or economic sense. We do not want material done in excessive scientific terminology. We welcome photo submissions (please write for list of upcoming topics), however, we cannot be responsible for submissions not accompanied by sufficient postage for return by certified mail. Payments are made for all material upon publication.

CHANGE OF ADDRESS: The post office does not automatically forward *Alaska Geographic*® when you move. To ensure continous service, notify us six weeks before moving. Send us your new address and zip code (and moving date), your old address and zip code, and if possible send a mailing label from a copy of *Alaska Geographic*®. Send this information to *Alaska Geographic*® Mailing Offices, 130 Second Avenue South, Edmonds, Washington 98020-3588.

MAILING LISTS: We have begun making our members' names and addresses available to carefully screened publications and companies whose products and activities might be of interest to you. If you would prefer not to receive such mailings, please so advise us, and include your mailing label (or your name and address if label is not available).

**About This Issue:** Alaska Natives and newcomers have used dogs and dogsleds for hundreds of years, first solely for transportation, later as the foundation for the state's official sport. For this issue, we called on *Anchorage Times* outdoor writer Bill Sherwonit, who brings together information on many aspects of dogs and dog mushing, including the history of dog racing, famous mushers, dog care, major dog races, sleds and equipment and raising and training sled dogs. Fairbanks writer and Yukon Quest dog musher Pete Bowers contributed material on the North American Championship, and added selected information on Northern dogs, the Yukon Quest and the early years of dog racing. Dorothy Page reviewed the manuscript.

We are grateful to the many photographers whose images capture the personalities of the dogs, the excitement of the races and the beauty of the trails.

The Library of Congress has cataloged this serial publication as follows:

Alaska Geographic. v.1-
[Anchorage, Alaska Geographic Society] 1972-
v. ill. (part col.). 23 x 31 cm.
Quarterly.
Official publication of the Alaska Geographic Society.
Key title: Alaska geographic, ISSN 0361-1353.

1. Alaska — Description and travel — 1959-
—Periodicals.  I. Alaska Geographic Society.

F901.A266     917.98′04′505     72-92087
                                        MARC-S
Library of Congress     75[7912]

Second Printing, 1989.

The sled dog and the North have always seemed synonymous and it is good to reflect that the sled dog of yesterday, who had almost slipped into anonymity with the arrival of the airplane in one age and the ski-mobile and three wheelers in another, is now enjoying new and growing stature.

True, where the sled dog of yesterday was mostly a necessary working accessory, and only from time to time a more glamorous sports figure, today he is perhaps even more coming to be recognized as "North" as Mounties, Klondike, and Robert Service.

More and more it has become a status symbol to own a big beautiful sharply masked malemute (or Husky if you will), but of all events in these changing times, the revival of the Iditarod Trail has served to make the Alaskan dog a television friend in a million living rooms and more than ever the Alaska symbol. And the Iditarod Race has even given greater prominence to the trail itself than it really was in early historical use. Actually, it was not so much an Anchorage to Nome trail (Anchorage wasn't even on the drawing boards when men and dogs were walking and driving the Iditarod) but it was mostly used by folks in the actual "Iditarod" country (Iditarod, Flat, Ophir, Takotna and other camps between the upper Kuskokwim and the middle Yukon).

Add another name to the list of men who achieved on the Iditarod Trail. My own uncle Ed Henning owned, at least for a time, the "walking out" championship time from the Iditarod to trail end at Seward.

The corroboration of that came to me from a really famed in his time Alaskan, the late Alexander Malcom "Sandy" Smith who, among other things claimed short time fame for leading the Standard Oil staking party to the Barrow oil seeps in about 1921 or thereabout.

Sandy told me he was having a miserable time one day with overflows everywhere and the dogs as miserable and wet as he was when my uncle Ed, a tall, rangy sort came walking by on his way to Knik and Seward,

leaving Sandy and his poor dogs soon behind.

One more recollect. Uncle Ed also told me that Nellie Neal's (later "Lawing") roadhouse on Kenai Lake, was the best on the route. Nellie was thoughtful enough to have a fish net stretched over the big cooking stove. Weary and wet travelers only had to throw their sodden socks up on the net to pick them up in the morning nice and dry.

To all trail dog lovers, and the Iditarod Trail itself, good to see you back. You are proof the real Alaska will never die.

*Robert A. Henning*

President,
The Alaska Geographic Society

# Northern Dogs

He who gives time to the study of the history of Alaska, learns that the dog, next to man, has been the most important factor in its past and present development.

Alaskan Judge James Wickersham, *Old Yukon: Tales, Trails and Trials* (1938)

Since nomadic tribes from Siberia first crossed the now-submerged Bering Land Bridge and set foot in Alaska, the people of the Great Land probably have relied heavily on man's best friend.

Evidence from 4,500 years ago (from eastern Canada and Greenland), and perhaps as far back as 11,500 years ago (in the Yukon Territory and Idaho), places man and dog together. Since their domestication in prehistoric times, dogs have played the role of companion, pet, guard, hunter, herder, worker and athlete. They've been used historically by trappers, explorers, mail carriers, gold miners, judges, clergymen, the military and, since the early 1900s, by racers.

No one knows for certain when people first used dogs to pull sleds. It seems likely that the idea of hitching dogs to sleds first originated among the native people of northern Eurasia. The idea probably spread quickly, and eventually found its way across the Bering Sea into Alaska.

Although the use of sleds is probably many thousand years old, the use of dogs for pulling sleds has most likely been practiced for not more than 1,500 years by prehistoric Eskimos of northern Alaska. The earliest indisputable archaeological evidence for this comes from the Kobuk River and Kotzebue area, where various sled parts and other evidence of dog

*Two canine members of a climbing party stand watch at camp on Ruth Glacier.*
(J. Schultz)

*A drawing done by John Webber, official artist for Captain Cook's third voyage (1776-1780), shows the simple leather thong used as a harness by the earliest dog mushers.* (From John Ledyard's journal; reprinted from *Racing Alaskan Sled Dogs,* 1976)

harnessing has been found in sites more than 300 years old.

Wherever dog mushing actually originated, it is clear that it was firmly established among the Eskimos of northern North America when the first white explorers arrived. The Eskimos of the coastal regions used dogs to pull sleds similar to modern sleds. Interior Athabascans, although they used toboggans pulled by people, most likely did not make extensive use of dogs for pulling until after contact with Russian explorers.

Early white explorers to Alaska offered firsthand accounts of native dogs. Henry M. Bannister, member of an expedition to Alaska from 1865 to 1867, observed, "The dogs were characterized by a bushy tail, erect ears and intelligent expression of countenance."

Bannister also noted that the dogs showed great enthusiasm for their sled-pulling tasks. "As soon as the sled is brought out . . . the dogs gather round, and, fairly dancing with excitement, raise their voices in about a dozen unmelodious strains."

The Natives Bannister encountered normally used five to seven dogs in a team. And as soon as they were able to travel, pups were included in the team, to learn pulling techniques from the older dogs. Rather than riding behind the sled, the Eskimo drivers ran ahead of the team to show the way and break trail. The use of whip and voice commands was "almost unknown among Alaskan Esquimaux," according to Bannister.

Because the Eskimos used their dogs for work, pulling power was more important than speed. The dogs were large, weighing 50 to 80 pounds on the average, with powerful physiques, heavy necks and chests, and short but strong legs. Leaders, however, were picked more for their intelligence, common sense and willingness to work than for their strength or size.

The teams were capable of pulling loads that averaged up to 75 pounds per dog, and sometimes more. Bannister saw one team of eight dogs travel 40 miles in one day, with a load of reindeer meat weighing 800 pounds. Including the weight of the sled, the team pulled about 1,000 pounds, or about 125 pounds per dog.

The native dogs, like their masters, endured a difficult life. They had to survive periods of starvation and many succumbed to the combined effects of hard

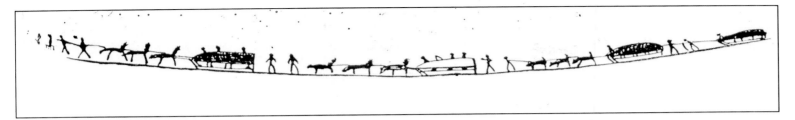

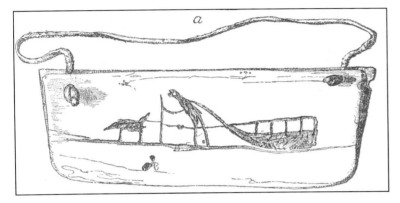

Graphic representations of dogs and dog sleds are often found on Eskimo artifacts. At left is a depiction of a piece of an old snow shovel, incised with the figures of a man and dog pulling an empty sled. The illustration above, carved on an ivory bucket handle, shows teams of dogs pulling a procession of loaded sleds.
(Both from *Graphic Art of the Eskimos*, Smithsonian Institution, 1897)

BELOW: *Dogs wait patiently while Natives load a skin boat frame onto a sled for the 35- to 40-mile run to Sealing Point, northwest of Kotzebue. Natives visit the point each spring to hunt seals and render seal oil.*
(Nichols Collection, courtesy of Mark Ocker, reprinted from *ALASKA GEOGRAPHIC*®)

work and scarce food. During the summer season, the dogs were often allowed to roam free and forage for their own food.

In winter, the Eskimos paid closer attention to the dogs' well-being. The normal diet included seal and walrus meat, although any available meat was used when necessary.

White man's arrival in Alaska brought about expanded use of dogs. Sled dog teams were used at different times by explorers, trappers, hunters, miners and mail carriers from the 18th century until the first half of the 20th century.

ABOVE: *Two outdoorsmen near Big Fish Lake, in the Brooks Range, enjoy ski-joring, a sport in which a person on skis is pulled by a horse, vehicle, or, in this case, a dog team.* (Stuart Pechek)

RIGHT: *Village dogs gather on the bank of the Yukon River at Fort Yukon, hoping for a free meal from a passing boat.*
(The Anchorage Museum)

# Northern Breeds

When thinking of northern dogs, the breeds most likely to come to mind are the Siberian husky, Alaskan malamute and Samoyed. Although the original inhabitants of North America may have used jackal-type dogs, northern breeds probably developed from the wolf. These dogs may have accompanied ancestral Eskimos into Alaska as early as 3500 B.C. Following centuries of cross-breeding, perhaps with arctic wolves, northern dogs developed individual characteristics and gradually evolved into what are called today the northern breeds.

The importance of dogs to the existence of northern Natives cannot be too strongly emphasized. For thousands of years dogs have been living and hunting with Natives, aiding in their daily survival. Dog fur may have been used for warm clothing, and evidence exists that some cultures even relied on the animals as a source of food.

The Alaskan malamute takes its name from the probable developers of the breed, the Mahlemut Eskimos of Alaska, a people known for their kindness to their dogs. The malamute is considered a natural breed, not the result of deliberate cross-breeding. The dogs are an example of survival of the fittest — produced by a long, continuous process of selecting only those dogs able to work and survive in a harsh northern environment. It is difficult to say when the breed was first developed, but American and Russian writers in the 19th century described the Mahlemut people and the high quality sled dogs they bred.

Largest of the sled dogs, the malamute is a hardy, thick-coated, powerful animal bred for harness work. It is also a quiet, affectionate and gentle dog, with an impressive sense of dignity. The malamutes' ability to withstand cold is legendary; they can be kept outdoors, under severe temperature conditions, with a minimum of shelter. The breed received official recognition by the American Kennel Club (AKC) in the 1930s.

The AKC standard for the Alaskan malamute requires it to be a powerful and substantially built dog with a thick, coarse guard coat and a dense, wooly undercoat.

*Quinyon, a 13-year-old malamute, surveys visitors to Sheep Mountain Lodge along the Glenn Highway. The dog's owner, Diane Schneider, explains that the unusual name comes from Vietnam, where the owner of Quinyon's father was once a USO entertainer.* (Penny Rennick, staff)

Face markings are either caplike, masklike or a combination, and colors range from light grey to black. The head is broad, ears wedge-shaped and erect when alerted. The position of the eyes gives a wolflike appearance, but the expression is soft. Blue eyes are cause for disqualification. The tail is plumed and carried over the back. The malamute is affectionate, friendly, loyal and playful, but dignified when mature.

**LEFT:** *The Alaskan malamute is the only purebred registered native Alaskan dog. Recognized by the American Kennel Club more than 50 years ago, the malamute is judged primarily on its ability as a sled dog for heavy freight. Shown here is Champion Kee-Too's Tundra Tracker, owned by Kay Moustakis of Anchorage.*
(Richard Hansen, courtesy of Kay Moustakis)

**RIGHT:** *A sprint dog, lean and sleek, awaits the start of a race. At 40 to 45 pounds, sprint dogs tend to be smaller than long-distance dogs, which generally weigh between 45 and 55 pounds.* (Bill Sherwonit)

**BELOW:** *Gayl Jokiel of Anchorage enjoys a run with her team of Samoyeds.*
(Courtesy of Gayl Jokiel)

*A 10-week-old malemute frolics in a patch of
dwarf dogwood.* (J. Schultz)

*Fanciers of Samoyeds, possibly the oldest of the arctic sled dogs, claim that this breed is most nearly akin to primitive dogs and that there has been no crossing of wolf or fox in the breed. Here, Kondako's Morningsong, owned by Gayl Jokiel of Anchorage, stands in proper show pose.* (Courtesy of Gayl Jokiel)

The Samoyed, named for the nomadic Samoyede people of the Siberian Arctic, is among the world's oldest known breeds. These dogs could be counted upon to act as hunters, reindeer herders, sled pullers and even child tenders.

The Samoyedes' close working and personal relationships with their dogs — the children were allowed to play with the pups and often the dogs were let into the warm reindeer skin tents to sleep — made them different from other Eskimo cultures. Native reluctance, and often refusal, to sell their dogs to 18th and 19th century explorers and traders further indicates the high regard they had for their animals.

The breed first became widely known to the western world when Norwegian explorer Fridtjof Nansen relied on teams of Samoyeds during his 1893 expedition to the North Pole. For his 1911 trek to the South Pole, another Norwegian, Roald Amundsen, selected Samoyeds for their intelligence, endurance, ingenuity and strength.

The AKC standard for the Samoyed calls for it to be of medium size, substantial yet agile in build, with a wedge-shaped head, dark almond-shaped eyes, well-furred erect ears and a smiling expression. It carries its tail over its back. Its thick stand-off coat may be pure white, cream, biscuit or a combination. Any other colors disqualify, as do blue eyes. In the show ring the Samoyed is gaited at an efficient, ground-covering trot to demonstrate correct conformation. Its gentle, intelligent, eager disposition is an important breed characteristic.

Perhaps the best known of all the northern breeds is the Siberian husky. "Husky," taken from a slang word for Eskimo, was first used generally for all sled dog breeds.

Evidence suggests that huskies were first hitched to sleds in northern Eurasia more than 500 years ago. Needing a speedy and

*The pup above has the bright blue eyes often associated with purebred Siberian huskies. The dog below shows how mixing breeds can result in eyes of different colors.* (Both by Alissa Crandall)

dependable means of transportation, the Natives used their dogs primarily for hauling game-laden sleds and in helping to move camp.

Siberians, once known for their remarkable racing ability, first gained attention in 1909 when a team of nine came in third in the 408-mile All Alaska Sweepstakes Race. Odds were 100 to one against the team and had they won, it is said their winning would have broken the Bank of Nome.

The Siberian husky is alert, graceful and strongly built. A number of desirable traits makes the breed good stock for racing dogs. Instinctively efficient hunters, huskies bark when they sight game. In addition, they are gentle, protective and loyal.

The AKC standard for the Siberian husky states that it be of medium size, quick and light on its feet, and free and graceful in action. Body proportions and form must reflect a basic balance of power, speed and great endurance. Colors range from black to pure white. The body is well-furred with erect ears, a trailing tail and almond-shaped eyes. Eyes may be brown, blue, one of each or parti-colored (brown and blue in the same eye). The Siberian husky is friendly, gentle, alert and outgoing with a measure of reserve and dignity expected in the mature dog. Its intelligence and obedient and eager disposition make it an agreeable companion and a willing worker.

*Earl Norris drives his team of Siberians in the World Championship race in 1985. Norris looks for the fastest dogs with the best conformation, believing that if a dog does not move properly it has to work harder to maintain speed.* (Bill Sherwonit)

ABOVE: *Turk (left) and Skookum, shown here in 1956, came from the kennel of Dorothy and Everett Wilde. When they were school teachers in Tetlin, the Wildes hauled mail with their dog team. In the 1950s and 1960s the mixed-breed dogs were used in local races and in weight-pulling contests in Fairbanks. These large dogs (Turk weighed about 90 pounds) were whelped by Missy, a female in Chuck O'Leary's search and rescue team in Nome.* (Everett Wilde)

*John Suter of Chugiak has the only racing team of poodles in Alaska. Nine years of training have resulted in wins in five of the 17 races the team has entered. Because of the poodles' endurance, pulling power, speed and adjustment to the climate, Suter hopes to enter the team in a future Iditarod race.* (Courtesy of John Suter)

*Considered one of the finest sled dog breeds, Mackenzie River huskies were used by the Royal North West Mounted Police for their long winter patrols in the early 1900s. They were also frequently used as freighting and mail dogs. Identified by their broad shoulders, deep chests and long legs, Mackenzie River huskies are a mixture of Eskimo dog, wolf and larger breeds such as Newfoundland and Saint Bernard.* (Richard Harrington)

*Joyce Wells poses with her Targhee hounds in 1953. Originally bred in Idaho, these dogs are a cross between staghounds and Irish setters. Fast sprint dogs, Targhees still occasionally appear in their pure form on dog teams in the West.* (The Anchorage Museum)

**ABOVE:** *A youngster in Nondalton spends his playtime with some frisky friends.* (Alissa Crandall)

**LEFT:** *Eskimo dogs, also called Greenland Eskimo dogs, range from Greenland to Labrador and other parts of northeastern North America. Used for centuries as a draft animal, the large-boned Eskimo dog has a powerful body, intelligence, good nature and the ability to withstand extreme cold. No longer recognized by the American Kennel Club, the Eskimo dog was dropped in the 1960s due to lack of interest among breeders.* (Richard Harrington)

Canadian trapper George Lush poses north of Eskimo Point, Northwest Territories, in 1950 with one of his Eskimo dogs. These huge, strong dogs have thick coats which enable them to withstand unlimited cold.
(Richard Harrington)

17

# Working Dogs

The abundance of fur-bearing animals in Alaska lured trappers and hunters. By the mid-1800s, the Hudson's Bay Company had reached Alaska's Interior and set up a trading post at Fort Yukon. The trappers traveled by boat in summer and dog-powered toboggans and sleds in winter. The teams — usually consisting of four dogs — were called dog trains; when two or more teams traveled together, the trains were combined into dog brigades.

Samuel Hearne, using teams of northern dogs, journeyed on three Hudson's Bay Company expeditions in Canada between 1769 and 1772, following the Coppermine River to the Arctic Ocean in search of a northwest passage to the Orient.

Another explorer, Thomas Simpson, traveled more than 1,900 miles with dogs during one two-month trek in northern Canada. Simpson's dogs were freighting breeds, accustomed to long hours in harness on all sorts of trails and in all kinds of weather. The dogs traveled an average of 25 to 30 miles a day.

Robert Kennicott, who explored the Interior in the early 1860s, kept a journal describing his adventures as a "dog team voyageur." Kennicott wrote that such voyageurs would on occasion travel up to 50 miles in a day.

Near the end of the 19th century, Alaska's gold miners put dogs to work in the winter hauling loads of freight.

*These burly canines haul laundry for Pioneer Steam Laundry in Anchorage in 1916.* (The Anchorage Museum)

*Dogs were a valuable commodity in Nome during the gold rush, when strong pullers could sell for $1,000 or more.*
(Courtesy of Ethel Becker; reprinted from The ALASKA JOURNAL®)

Freighters, called "dog punchers," made a living using dogs to deliver food, supplies, mail and mining equipment to claims, and to pack out the gold.

The size of the loads varied with the size of individual dogs and the team as a whole. In general, punchers would haul loads equal to one and one-half times the weight of the team. Thus big, strong dogs were preferred. Such dogs were soon in short supply and dogs of every size, shape and description were put to work in front of freight sleds.

As the demand for dogs increased, so did the price — a big, strong durable dog could sell for $1,000 or more. Soon, as local supply dwindled, a canine black market developed in the Lower 48. Dogs were bought or stolen and then brought to Alaska and sold to miners and freighters at inflated prices. Often the dogs were interbred with native dogs to produce Alaskan huskies of every description. Dogs were shipped from seaports as far down the West Coast as Los Angeles.

"It was said that no dog larger than a spaniel was safe on the streets of Seattle, or San Francisco, or Los Angeles, during the northern Gold Rush," wrote Lorna Coppinger in *The World of Sled Dogs* (1977).

By the 1890s, sled dogs had become important to the mail service. It could be said that neither blinding blizzards, nor subzero temperatures, nor 70-mph winds could keep the mushing mail carriers from

**ABOVE:** *A dog team tows a boat up the Snake River in this view made from an early post card. Miners congregated near the river's mouth at the turn of the century seeking the yellow prize, gold.*
(The Anchorage Museum)

**RIGHT:** *The first winter mail leaves Anchorage by dog team November 28, 1916.*
(The Anchorage Museum)

JOHNSON AND JEPSEN GENERAL MERCHANDISE

HOWA

MODEL CAFÉ

ROOM

CAFÉ

CAPE'S HOUS TIN SHOP ROOMS

U.S. MAIL CARRIER JACK LAMONT'S RACING TEAM RUBY, ALASKA. 1916
WINNER OF THE 1915 RUBY DERBY

**LEFT:** *Jack LaMont, U.S. Mail carrier at Ruby on the Yukon River, won the 1915 Ruby Derby, with this racing team.* (Courtesy of Earl Norris)

**BELOW:** *Northern dogs were used for recreation in the early days of the territory just as they are now. This team has joined several Nome residents for a romp on the Bering Sea ice in 1910. One dog, named Casey, enjoys the freedom of a pet and roams the ice hummock at lower right.*
(The Anchorage Museum)

their appointed rounds. Speedy delivery of mail to Alaska's gold-boom communities was so crucial that a federal law required all other sled dog drivers to give the right of way to any mail-carrying team encountered along the trail.

The peak of dog-team mail delivery lasted from about 1910 into the 1930s. Mail to the Interior was carried on a Valdez-to-Fairbanks route. Also important was the Iditarod Trail, actually a system of trails that stretched more than 2,000 miles from Seward to Nome. Communities served by the main route included Knik, McGrath, Flat, Iditarod, Unalakleet, Golovin and Solomon. Side routes went to Anchorage, Hope, Ruby, Koyukuk, Galena and several other villages and towns.

The Iditarod Trail was strictly a winter route. Boats and barges provided necessary transportation during the summer when the trail was impassable because of tundra

*After Nome's Wild Goose Railroad ceased operating around 1910, local residents continued running an assortment of vehicles on the tracks. Here a "pupmobile" carries two passengers along the line.*
(The ALASKA JOURNAL®)

bogs and swamps. But once winter set in, dogs took over the mail delivery.

Pete Curran, who inherited the Nome-Golovin mail contract from his father in the

BELOW: *Lee Damron fishes in the Swanson River, on the Kenai Peninsula, as Thor, a German shepherd-collie mix, remains on the lookout for wildlife.* (Alissa Crandall)

RIGHT: *These dogs can pull a roller just as easily as a wagon or sled. The grooming squad welcomes the dogs to their crew while smoothing the field of a ball park in Anchorage in 1916.* (The Anchorage Museum)

"Dog-gone" good roller
Ball Park
Anchorage Alaska
gee photo

*Rangers in Denali National Park and Preserve have used dogs since the early 1920s, when rangers were assigned teams of dogs and districts to patrol. Here, one-time ranger Fritz Nyberg prepares a meal at the park with the help of his canine friend.*
(The Anchorage Museum)

Patsy Ann Official Greeter of Juneau, Alaska — Meets All Boats.

LEFT: "Official greeter" on the Juneau docks in the 1930s was Patsy Ann, a pit bull terrier. According to locals the dog met every arriving ship, looking for her master who had left town on a boat; Patsy Ann survived on handouts from the ships' galley workers. (Lucile McDonald; reprinted from ALASKA GEOGRAPHIC®)

BELOW: Jeff Schultz and his dog, Kodiak, pause along the trail to take in a waterfall in the Talkeetna Mountains. (J. Wright)

Mark Kirchhoff of Port Alexander relates the story of Riley, the panhandling pooch. Riley frequented the local pub, panhandling the customers for nickels, with which he would buy chocolate bars from the bartender. According to the story, Riley was able to tell the difference between nickels and coins of other denominations by feeling them between his teeth. He would spit out anything but a nickel, the price of his candy bar. (Courtesy of Mark Kirchhoff; reprinted from The ALASKA JOURNAL®)

1920s, ran his dog team along the mail route six days a week, from late November until the first of May.

"It took me three days to get to Golovin and three days to get back," he said. He usually ran a team of 21 to 23 dogs. His mail-carrier days ended in 1938, when Pan American Airlines won the contract for the Nome-Golovin route.

Mail-delivery dogs were bred and built for hard work, as their loads typically weighed several hundred pounds. Charlie Biederman, who delivered mail in the 1930s between Eagle City and Circle City in Alaska's Interior, said his wheel dog was "part German shepherd and weighed 110 pounds," about twice the size of a racing dog in the 1980s.

Like Curran, Biederman lost his contract to an airline, Wien. That was the eventual fate of nearly all dog-team mail carriers in the 1920s and 1930s as air transportation replaced mushing as the primary means of travel and mail delivery to Alaska's bush communities.

In 1963, the last U.S. Postal Service mail driver, Chester Noongwook of Savoonga, on St. Lawrence Island, retired his dog team. The replacement: an airplane, naturally.

*Steve Melchor and his dogs haul brush for Steve's pet moose, Elsie, at Seward. Long-time resident of the Kenai Peninsula, Steve had a moose ranch on the Kenai until a flood of the Snow River inundated the ranch. Steve managed to save all but one of his moose from the raging waters, but afterwards all the moose escaped to the woods except Elsie. Steve moved to Seward where he and Elsie were prime tourist attractions. When Elsie reached adult size, Steve sold the moose to the Belle Isle Zoo in Detroit and went along with her as caretaker.* (The Anchorage Museum)

*Bill Vaudrin (center, facing camera), Gus Vaudrin (at left) and two unidentified companions mush back to Pedro Bay, at the northeast end of Iliamna Lake, after a spring meeting at Iliamna village.*
(Don and Lorene Stump)

# Sleds and Equipment

Dog mushers use a variety of sleds, with function determining the exact style, width, length and weight. For instance, sprint racers, who emphasize speed, tend to prefer lightweight sleds, usually weighing 20 to 25 pounds. But there's a corresponding sacrifice in sled strength. Long-distance mushers, seeking increased strength and durability, opt for heavier sleds.

Yet for all the differences in use and needs, dogsleds show a remarkable similarity in style. To the uninitiated, there

*This photo shows a basic Yukon sled, widely used in the Interior by miners, trappers and hunters. Merchants such as the Northern Commercial Company sold the bottom portion and runners of the sleds; each owner added his own handlebars and basket.* (Eagle Historical Society)

*The most common mechanical brake on a racing sled consists of a pronged piece of metal, held up by springs. The brake is applied by stepping on it, forcing the claws into the snow.* (Con Bunde)

**BELOW:** *Greenland-style sleds, such as this model, are among the earliest sleds used by North American Eskimos. This type of sled averages 14 feet in length and today is generally made of well-seasoned hardwood, sealed with paint or varnish. The size and strength of Greenland sleds and the width of the runners make them excellent for use on rough terrain and jagged sea ice.*
(University of Alaska Museum, Fairbanks)

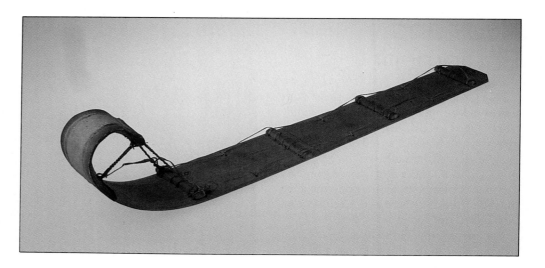

**RIGHT:** *Toboggans, made of bent wood or birch bark, are best for use in soft, deep snow and in wooded areas. These sleds are lighter than other types and are able to withstand rough treatment. Athabascans of interior Alaska and Canada commonly used toboggans similar to this model made in the Yukon River village of Rampart.*
(University of Alaska Museum, Fairbanks)

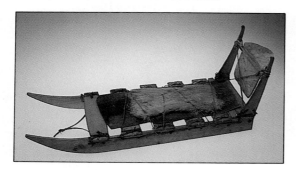

*The most widely used type of sled is the basket sled, made from hardwood and lashed together with sinew, rawhide or nylon cord. Basket sleds are used for carrying passengers, light freight or for racing. This model of a racing sled was made by Steve Nathaniel of Circle.*
(University of Alaska Museum, Fairbanks)

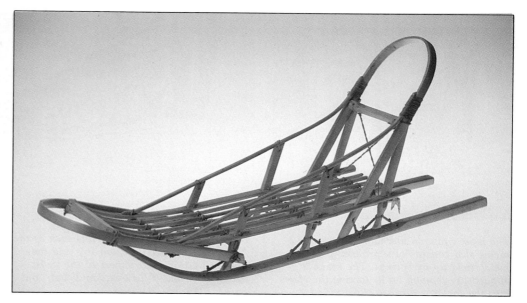

is little to distinguish one sled from another. In fact, there is little to separate today's wooden sleds from those perfected by mushers of the early 1900s.

A wooden racing sled includes certain basic components: a basket, the body or chassis in which equipment, food, people and tired or injured dogs are transported; runners, the pieces on which the sled glides; handlebars, which the driver holds onto; the brush bow, a curved piece in front of the sled to help ward off obstacles; and the brake, a pronged piece of metal attached to a board at the bottom of the sled for slowing or stopping the rig along the trail.

Although some sled builders and mushers have experimented with other materials such as metal and plastic, most sleds are still made from hardwood, preferably hickory.

Sleds are neither factory built nor mass produced, but are the products of craftsmen, who make them one at a time. The most time-consuming part of building a sled is bending the thin strips of wood into the shapes needed for the finished product. To gain the needed curvature, sled builders soften the wood by putting the strips in hot water or steam and then placing them in special forms which give the wood the desired bend.

Once the pieces have been prepared, the sled is lashed together. The parts are normally tied together, rather than nailed, screwed or glued, to improve the sled's flexibility. Traditionally, reindeer sinew or

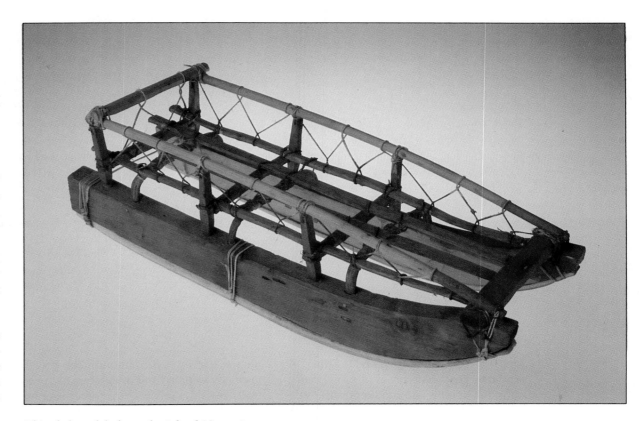

*This sled model, from the inland Nunamiut Eskimos of Anaktuvuk Pass, is typical of the "built-up" sled. The heavy, wide runners, traditionally fashioned from whalebone or driftwood, were well-suited to travel over rough terrain. Similar styles are known to have come from the Yukon-Kuskokwim delta, St. Lawrence Island, Kotzebue and across western Alaska. The model was made by Frank Akmalik of Tulugak Valley, in the Brooks Range.*
(University of Alaska Museum, Fairbanks)

*George Beck hauls wood on a pair of bobsleds hitched to a team.*
(Eagle Historical Society)

rawhide was used to tie a sled together. A modern replacement is nylon cord, although some sled-makers still use rawhide. The wood is typically coated with lacquer, varnish or oil for added protection.

Strips of plastic or metal are added to the bottom of the runners to protect the wood and improve the sled's glide. Often wax is applied to match the temperature and snow conditions.

On modern sleds, ends of the runners extend behind the sled for the musher to stand on. Such extensions were not present on the earliest sleds, because the driver normally went in front of the team to break trail. For the same reason, there were no handlebars at the back of the earliest sleds.

The dogs are hooked up to the sled by harnesses and a variety of lines. A harness made of cotton, nylon or leather webbing is worn by each dog; the harness should put the strain of pulling on the dog's shoulders and chest and allow as much freedom as possible. Ideally, each harness is custom-fit to the individual dog. Racing harnesses, much lighter than freight harnesses, weigh about two ounces.

The main line running out from the sled to the dog team is called the towline or gangline and is generally made of braided nylon or plastic rope. The double-tandem towline, to which dogs are hooked up in pairs, has become standard for sled dog racers.

A different sort of hook-up, used by Alaskan Natives and mushers in earlier times (and still used by the Inuit of eastern

*This diagram shows the configuration of the double tandem hitch, the most versatile hitching arrangement. The double tandem is popular with mushers because the short lines do not snag or tangle easily and the dogs break two trails, in which the sled runners follow.*

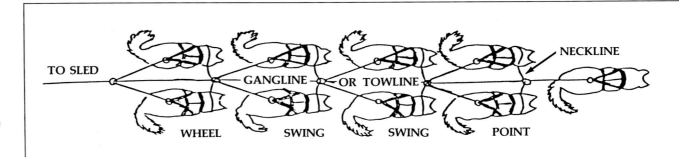

TO SLED

NECKLINE

GANGLINE OR TOWLINE

WHEEL    SWING    SWING    POINT

*Long-distance mushers often make adaptations to their sleds to provide more comfort. At left, Terry Adkins has equipped his sled with modern handlebars; above, Jan Masek has added a bicycle seat.*
(Left, J. Schultz; above, Ron Wendt)

33

*The Inuit of eastern Canada and Greenland*
*use a different type of harnessing*
*arrangement, called a fan hitch.*
(Richard Harrington)

Canada and Greenland), is called a fan hitch because the dogs are tied by separate lines to the sled and allowed to fan out. The fan hitch allows the dogs freedom of movement, but is seldom used today because of the tendency for lines to become tangled, and, as each dog must break his own trail, the team tires quickly.

All dogs except the leaders are hooked up by lines tied to the harness, through which the dogs' pulling power is transferred to the towline and thus the sled.

A musher may carry a variety of other gear, such as snow hook or anchor, made of steel and embedded in the ice or snow to stop the team; booties, designed to protect the dogs' feet from injury; a whip, usually cracked above the dogs to increase the team's speed; a jingler, a noisemaker made of bells or bottle caps and used by some mushers instead of a whip to make a team go faster; and a dog bag, placed in the basket to hold injured or tired dogs.

Mushers who run trap lines or compete in long-distance races carry additional equipment for winter survival in the outdoors. Mandatory gear for the Iditarod includes: cold-weather sleeping bag, ax, snowshoes, extra booties and extra food for the dogs.

*Warm clothing is a must for any musher. Susan Butcher's fur-lined mittens are emblazoned with the mushing commands for "right" and "left."* (J. Schultz)

*Pecos Humphrey of Talkeetna puts booties on one of his huskies prior to the start of the 1985 Don's Iditarod 200 race in Willow. Booties protect the dogs' feet from injury on icy and uneven trails.* (Bill Sherwonit)

# The Race For Life

The most important sled dog race in Alaska's history was not a sporting event — it was the diphtheria serum run of 1925.

The race included 20 drivers and more than 100 dogs who covered 674 miles "over some of the roughest, most desolate country in the world" in less than six days.

Their mission of mercy was to carry a 20-pound package of diphtheria antitoxin from Nenana to Nome, where a diphtheria outbreak threatened to become a fatal epidemic.

In mid-January, after a child died in Nome, Curtis Welch, the only doctor in the town of 1,439, diagnosed the cause of her death as diphtheria. Soon other children became infected and Welch sent out a desperate call for help, with telegraph messages to Fairbanks, Juneau, Seward and Anchorage. His supply of antitoxin was

*Ultimate destination of the mushers taking part in the 1925 race to rescue Nome from a growing diphtheria epidemic was Maynard Columbus Hospital.* (Carrie McLain Museum)

small, and Nome was the regional medical supply center for the 11,000 Natives threatened by the disease.

The nearest antitoxin supply was in Anchorage, where Dr. J.B. Beeson had 300,000 units at the Alaska Railroad Hospital. The problem was getting the serum to Nome in the shortest time possible. The first and most obvious choice was to fly the serum, using two airplanes available in Fairbanks, but the planes had been dismantled and stored for the winter.

Dog teams seemed the only reliable answer.

The serum was packaged in a cylinder, wrapped in an insulating quilt and tied in canvas. It was then shipped by train from Anchorage to Nenana, about 225 miles away.

Meanwhile, in Nome the commissioner of the city's Board of Health chose Leonhard Seppala to drive a team of dogs to Nulato to intercept the serum. Seppala selected 20 dogs for the trip. He planned to reach Nulato with eight dogs, dropping the other 12 along the way so that he would have fresh dogs to substitute for tired ones on the return trip. At the head of the team, he put his now-famous lead dog, Togo.

The epidemic began to spread at an alarming rate. Unknown to Seppala, already out on the trail, officials decided to speed up the serum by using a series of relay teams over short distances.

On January 27, the race began.

William "Wild Bill" Shannon, a mail driver with the Northern Commercial

*Leonhard Seppala's famous lead dog, Togo, was a direct descendent of the Siberians brought to Alaska in 1910 by musher Fox Maule Ramsay. Seppala found the dog to be a natural-born leader, and kept him a part of his team until Togo was retired at the age of 16.* (Carrie McLain Museum)

Company, took the serum when it arrived in Nenana. Driving a team of nine malemutes in minus-50-degree weather, he headed for Tolovana, 52 miles to the northwest.

At noon on January 28, Shannon passed the serum to Edgar Kallands. Kallands' nine-dog team covered the 31 miles to Manley Hot Springs in temperatures to minus 60.

Dan Green carried the serum to Fish Lake; Johnny Folger went on to Tanana, where it is likely that Sam Joseph took over and headed for Kallands. (**Editor's note:** Recent information from oral histories indicates that the commonly accepted account of the beginning segments of the serum run is incorrect. The following is now believed to be the order in which mushers carried the serum.) Although it is not known for certain, it is probable that Titus Nickolai then went on to Nine Mile Cabin, Dave Corning to Kokrines, and Harry Pitka fought whiteout conditions on his drive to Ruby.

With the temperature still at minus 40 or below, Bill McCarty took the serum from Ruby to Whiskey Creek; Edgar Nollner traveled to Galena; and Edgar's brother, George Nollner, mushed the same team to Bishop Mountain.

At Bishop Mountain, Charlie Evans took over and left for Nulato with the temperature plunging to minus 64-degrees. Two of Evans' dogs began freezing in the groin area and had to be loaded onto the

*Charlie Evans, one of the mushers for the 1925 diphtheria serum run to Nome, wears honorary bib No. 1 for the 1983 Iditarod race. Evans carried the serum from Bishop Mountain to Nulato in temperatures below minus-60 degrees.* (J. Schultz)

sled. Evans then ran in front, helping to pull the sled.

Tommy Patson carried the precious cargo to Kaltag, arriving at noon on January 30. In three days, 13 drivers and 12 teams had covered 377 miles.

At Kaltag, the trail left the Yukon River and headed over the mountains to the coast. An Athabascan Indian river pilot known only as Jackscrew drove his team in minus-50-degree temperatures from Kaltag to Old Woman, where an Eskimo

named Victor Anagick took over and carried the serum to Unalakleet. Another Eskimo, Myles Gonangan, then mushed his way through a coastal storm and had to break through waist-high drifts during the run to Shaktoolik.

At Shaktoolik, Henry Ivanoff took the serum. Only 12 miles out of the village, Ivanoff met Seppala, who had traveled 170 miles from Nome. Seppala turned around and returned to Issac's Point; then, after a rest, he continued on to Golovin, where he passed the cargo to Charlie Olson. For their part in the serum run, Seppala and his team traveled 260 miles — no other musher went more than 53 miles.

Olson fought his way through 50-mph winds and minus-30-degree temperatures to reach Bluff. Gunnar Kaason then took over, running the final 53 miles with 13 dogs in harness and Seppala's second-team dog, Balto, in the lead.

Kaason had been scheduled to relay the serum to Ed Rohn at Safety for the final 22-mile leg of the run. Instead, Kaason continued, reportedly because his team "was doing so well" and he didn't want to wake Rohn. Others, however, later accused Kaason of trying to gain publicity by being the musher to bring the serum into Nome.

On the final stretch, Kaason and his team ran into a severe blizzard and whiteout conditions. Kaason could barely see his wheel dogs (those closest to the sled) and lost track of his position, but Balto managed to keep the team on the trail.

At 5:30 a.m. on February 2, Kaason and his team of dogs, with bloody, torn feet, pulled into Nome to a hero's welcome. The serum had been frozen during the long, hard run, but was still effective.

Drivers who helped transport the serum received medals and certificates signed by President Coolidge. By race's end, the "Great Race of Mercy" had made headlines around the world and the mushers had become heroes. The biggest heroes of all were Kaason, Seppala, and his two lead dogs, Togo and Balto.

Although Seppala always maintained that Togo was the greater hero, newspapers worldwide carried praise for Balto. In a special tribute, a bronze statue of Balto was placed in New York City's Central Park, with the inscription, "Dedicated to the indomitable spirit of the sled dogs that relayed anti-toxin six hundred miles over rough ice, across treacherous waters, through arctic blizzards from Nenana to the relief of a stricken Nome in the winter of 1925. Endurance — fidelity — intelligence."

Years later, Seppala commented: "It was almost more than I could bear when the newspaper dog, Balto, received a statue in Central Park in New York for his accomplishments, decked out in Togo's colors, and with the claim that he had taken Amundsen to Point Barrow and part way to the North Pole, when he had never been 200 miles north of Nome."

*A statue honoring Balto, Leonhard Seppala's dog who led Gunnar Kaason's team on the final leg of the diphtheria serum run to Nome in 1925, stands in New York's Central Park.* (Peter Howe)

# Leonhard Seppala

Leonhard Seppala didn't grow up around sled dogs. He didn't drive a dog team until he was in his 20s, and he never entered a sled dog race until he was 36. Yet long before he died in 1967 at age 90, Seppala had become a legend as the greatest dog-team driver ever.

Seppala was born in Norway in 1877; he left his home at the turn of the century and headed to Alaska in pursuit of gold. Soon after arriving in Nome, however, he ended his gold-mining career and began working as a dog-

*Mushers line up a team in front of the hospital in Candle, on the northern edge of the Seward Peninsula. In one of many mercy missions undertaken by the famous musher, Leonhard Seppala brought the injured Bobby Brown here from the inland village of Dime Landing.*
(Courtesy of Thelma Glazounow)

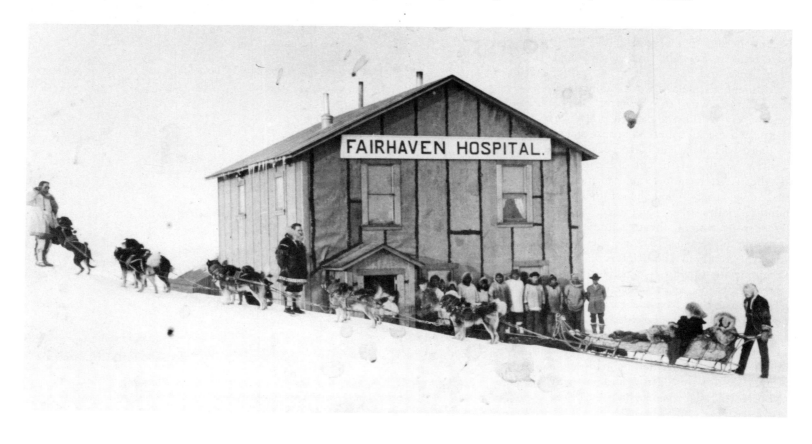

puncher, transporting supplies with a team of freight dogs. The sled dog racing fever eventually infected Seppala.

In 1913 he entered his first race, the Moose Burden Handicap, and he won. The following year, he was asked to train a group of Siberian huskies for explorer Roald Amundsen, who planned a sled dog trip to the North Pole. The trip fell through, but Seppala found another good use for the Siberians — he entered them in the All Alaska Sweepstakes.

Then came the 1915 sweepstakes, and the start of the Seppala legend. Another local legend, A.A. "Scotty" Allan, was favored to win the eighth annual sweepstakes. Allan had won three of the previous seven races, and had never finished lower than third. Allan was thought to be unbeatable, but Seppala outmushed the acknowledged master.

Many more victories followed. Seppala won numerous short races in the Nome area and extended his sweepstakes winning streak to three before the series ended in 1917.

Word of Seppala's mushing expertise soon spread to Alaska's Interior, and in 1916 members of the Ruby Kennel Club

issued a challenge to their Nome counterparts, inviting them to send a musher to compete in the Ruby Dog Derby. Seppala took up the challenge. In 11 days he drove his team more than 400 miles from Nome to Ruby, arriving several days before the race to learn the course and rest his dogs. When Derby Day finally arrived, Seppala not only beat the local talent, he broke the course record by more than eight minutes.

The following winter, Seppala added to his growing legend. After driving his 16-dog team to the community of Dime Landing, Seppala was greeted with a medical emergency. Miner Bobby

Brown had been badly injured in a sawmill accident, suffering from a broken arm, crushed ribs and a leg "nearly sawed off." Seppala was asked to transport Brown to Candle, about 60 miles away, because his was the best team in the country.

Seppala agreed to undertake the mission of mercy. Despite already tired dogs, an unfamiliar trail and getting caught in a blizzard, Seppala reached Candle in less than a half-day. Unfortunately, the desperate drive had been in vain. Three days after being admitted to the hospital in Candle, Brown died.

The best-known Seppala legend was

*Mushing legend Leonhard Seppala poses with his daughter, Sigrid, and his team of Siberian dogs in front of the queen's throne at the Fairbanks Ice Carnival in this 1930s photo.* (Alaska Northwest Publishing)

Winners of the Ruby Kennel Club's 1916 Ruby Derby. From Ruby, Alaska to Long And Return, 57½ Miles.

*Leonhard Seppala, winner of the 1916 Ruby Derby, poses with runners-up Charlie Frisco and George Jimie and four of the winning dogs.*
(Courtesy of Earl Norris)

born in 1925, when Seppala and his team played a critical role in the diphtheria serum run from Nenana to Nome.

After the serum run, Seppala toured the East Coast. And his teams won, just as they'd won in Alaska. When he wasn't racing, he was teaching others to race and raise Siberians. During the 1932 Winter Olympics at Lake Placid, New York, Seppala competed in the sled dog demonstration race, consisting of two 25-mile heats. He finished second, to Canadian Emil St. Godard.

Seppala returned to Alaska in the mid-1930s. After his retirement from mushing, he moved to Seattle, where he died in 1967.

Despite all his accomplishments, Seppala remains best known for the manner in which he handled his dogs, with kindness and encouragement. Perhaps the best tribute to Seppala is the Iditarod Trail Sled Dog Race's annual Leonhard Seppala Humanitarian Award, given to the musher who demonstrates the most humane treatment and care of his dog team.

It's an award Seppala would have applauded wholeheartedly.

# Dogs and the Military

Shortly after the end of the sweepstakes series and the entry of the United States into World War I, more than 100 of Alaska's finest — sled dogs, of course — were recruited by the military.

At the beginning of the war, a couple of Nome residents left Alaska to join the French Army. Several months later one of those men, Lt. René Haas, contacted three-time sweepstakes winner Scotty Allan.

Haas requested that 100 sled dogs and all the necessary equipment be gathered for use in the Vosges Mountains of France, where men, horses and mules had become hopelessly bogged down in deep snow.

Allan began buying up the best dogs he could find in Nome and surrounding villages. By the time Haas returned to Alaska to oversee the shipment of Nome's canine corps, Allan had assembled 106 dogs plus sleds, harnesses and two tons of dried salmon.

The dogs left Nome aboard the SS *Senator*, then crossed Canada by rail. In Canada, Allan recruited another 300 dogs.

Finally, with more than 400 dogs in his command, Allan left Quebec for France.

The Alpine Chasseurs, the company with which Allan's dogs were to work, had no previous dog-handling experience but were soon taught how to harness the dogs and use the commands "gee," "haw," "whoa" and of course "mush," which began as the French command "marche." The

*A barge prepares to carry more than 100 dogs to the SS* Senator, *off the coast of Nome, during World War I. The animals were bound for eastern France to assist the French Army.* (Lomen Brothers; University of Alaska Archives, Fairbanks)

*A team of dogs, born and trained in Alaska, stands harnessed and waiting to go in the Vosges Mountains of France in 1918. The dogs hauled equipment and ammunition to units not reachable by other means. This photo originally appeared in* The New York Times, *August 18, 1918.* (NYT Pictures)

dogs were divided into 60 teams, with some reserved for packing, sentry or Red Cross duty.

The dogs proved their worth immediately. Pulling sleds loaded with a total of 90 tons of ammunition, they reached a French unit which had been cut off and isolated in the Vosges Mountains for two weeks.

On other missions, the dog teams were used to string more than 20 miles of telephone wire and to haul supplies and ammunition to units not reachable by other means. In addition, the dogs pulled sleds loaded with wounded men to field hospitals, thus helping to save lives.

The sled dogs became heroes. Their accomplishments were recorded and praised in newspapers on both sides of the Atlantic Ocean. Three dogs were decorated with the Croix de Guerre for valor in battle.

Alaskan sled dogs also played an important role both prior to and during World War II. In response to Japanese efforts during the 1930s to map details of Alaska's coastline, particularly the Aleutian Islands, Col. Marvin "Muktuk" Marston traveled thousands of miles by dog team while organizing a tundra army, the Alaska Territorial Guard.

During World War II, the U.S. Army

*In this painting by Colcord "Rusty" Heurlin, Col. Marvin "Muktuk" Marston mushes along the trail in 1942 during efforts to organize rural Alaskans for the Alaska Territorial Guard during World War II.*
(Courtesy of Wilda Marston)

*During and for many years following World War II, the military in Alaska maintained units for search and rescue missions. Dogs were often vital parts of these organizations, like the team shown here with Sergeant Jim Johnson, a member of the Air Corps Land Rescue crew.* (U.S. Army Signal Corps photo by Glen McCreary)

*An Army paratrooper and his companion "Paratrooper Joe" get ready to jump from a C-47 cargo plane on this simulated rescue maneuver, which probably took place in the early 1950s. According to Air Force files, this is Joe's fifth jump. The soldier and his dog were assigned to the 10th Rescue Squadron at Ladd Field, now Fort Wainwright, near Fairbanks.* (USAF)

developed sled dog units in which dogs and drivers were assigned for arctic rescues. The three main camps were stationed in Maine, Montana and Alaska. Army sled dog drivers used a War Department field manual titled "Dog Team Transportation," a product of the Army's experience with working sled dogs in Alaska.

In February 1943 Norman Vaughan — who had mushed teams during Richard Byrd's Antarctic expedition of 1928 to 1930 and later moved to Alaska and raced in both the Iditarod and the North American — was assigned to organize an arctic search and rescue unit. Most of Vaughan's dogs were recruited from New England, but many of the two dozen dog drivers to join "Vaughan's Rangers" had gained their mushing experience in Alaska. The dogs and their drivers conducted numerous rescue missions from 1943 to 1945.

Joe Redington Sr. served in the post-war military forces in Alaska. From 1949 until 1957 the future "Father of the Iditarod"

worked as a civilian for the Air Force, using his dog teams to salvage planes that had crashed in remote, mountainous areas and to rescue the survivors or recover the remains of those involved in such crashes.

# Sled Dogs and the Mountain

Sled dogs played an integral role in early climbs of Mount McKinley. A dog team hauled supplies from Fairbanks to Muldrow Glacier, at the 11,000-foot level, for the four-man Sourdough Expedition of 1910. Three of the climbers — William Taylor, Pete Anderson and Charles McGonagall — decided to launch a one-day summit attempt from there. McGonagall turned back 500 feet from the top. Taylor and Anderson continued on, however, reaching the summit of the shorter North Peak and returning to camp in the same day, without any accidents. For food, they carried nothing more than a thermos of hot chocolate and a half-dozen doughnuts each.

In June 1913 a four-man team led by Hudson Stuck, Episcopal Archdeacon of the Yukon, reached the 20,320-foot summit of McKinley. In mid-March the four-man expedition had used dog teams to relay one and one-half tons of food, firewood and gear 50 miles, from the north side to the base of the mountain.

Stuck's expedition then drove a team to the head of Muldrow Glacier, from

*An ice bridge enables Earl Norris and his dog team to haul a freight sled across a crevasse on Muldrow Glacier during Bradford Washburn's 1947 ascent of Mount McKinley.* (Bradford Washburn, reprinted from A Tourist Guide to Mount McKinley)

where the climbers ferried loads to intermediate camps. Finally, on June 7, they left their camp at 17,500 feet and struggled to the top.

Although dog teams have been used to support a number of expeditions, only once have dogs actually been mushed to the top of North America's highest peak.

The historic climb occurred in May 1979 when mushers Joe Redington Sr. and Susan Butcher drove a team of four dogs to McKinley's summit.

The mushers, with seven dogs, began their expedition in late April at the 7,500-foot base camp on Kahiltna Glacier. Guided by Ray Genet and Brian Okonek, they followed the West Buttress, least difficult of the mountain's climbing routes. Twice during the seven-week trip the mountaineers and their dogs were forced to hole up by winds that reached 100 mph. Three of the dogs balked at the 14,500-foot level and were left with another party. The most difficult section was at Windy Corner, where Genet tied the dogs to climbing lines to ensure against a fall. The dogs, however, "had little problem keeping their feet."

The team finally reached the summit on Memorial Day, in 25- to 30-degree weather with clear skies and no wind.

Redington called the climb "the toughest trip I ever took" and later vowed he would never again try climbing the mountain with a dog team. "You just can't keep up with them," he said. "They're too strong. Look at them. They look better now than when we left."

*In spring 1979, mushers Susan Butcher and Joe Redington Sr., photographer Rob Stapleton and guide Ray Genet took a team of huskies to the top of 20,320-foot Mount McKinley. It was the first such trip to include dog teams. Here, Butcher relays supplies over a relatively flat stretch at the 12,300-foot level of McKinley's West Buttress.* (Brian Okonek)

*Nearly encased in windblown snow, a dog team rests peacefully at the 17,300-foot level of Mount McKinley during a successful 1979 climb to the top.* (Brian Okonek)

ABOVE: *A pair of mushers guides a freighting team along the crest of Stony Ridge in Denali National Park. The sleds hold supplies for climbing teams.* (Brian Okonek)

RIGHT: *Tom Lloyd, Pete Anderson, Charley McGonagall and Bill Taylor, members of the Sourdough Expedition, attempted to climb the North Peak of Mount McKinley's summit in 1910. This illustration shows Tom Lloyd and his lead dogs coming off the mountain April 11, 1910.* (Reprinted from *The ALASKA JOURNAL®*)

ABOVE: *Despite a light snowfall in September 1980, tourists at Denali National Park and Preserve attend the sled dog demonstration. The dogs are the park's most popular attraction, drawing some 30,000 visitors each year.* (George Wuerthner; reprinted from *ALASKA GEOGRAPHIC®*)

# Seal Dogs

Ringed seals remain one of the Arctic's mysteries, challenging biologists who must enter the frigid world of northern ice to learn about these mammals. The seals are seldom seen because they live only on arctic ice or in the water. But, with the use of dogs, scientists are knocking on the ringed seals' door.

Clyde is one of those special dogs. When John Burns, a former Alaska Department of Fish and Game biologist, moves his research team onto the ice in November, Clyde is right there to do his part. Clyde and other seal dogs run in front of a snow machine, their nose into the wind, searching for the smell of ringed seals. These marine mammals live in lairs one to four feet under the snow and make holes in the ice to breathe. When a dog detects seal odor, it runs to the spot and begins digging. The handler digs through to open the lair and allows the dog to sniff around to reinforce the scent. These dogs' senses of smell are so acute that they can locate ringed seal lairs up to one-half mile away in windy conditions, but more commonly their quarry is one-eighth to one-fourth mile distant.

Eskimos have been using dogs to locate seal holes for centuries. After the hunter and his dog found the first hole, the Eskimo would locate all the other breathing holes in a particular area and either station a

*Clyde and BW are all set to give biologist Bob Nelson a ride in search of ringed seal lairs.*
(Kathy Frost)

*Having detected seal odor, Clyde immediately follows the scent to a ringed seal lair. Here Clyde is digging into the lair. The yellow lab was trained in Canada by Dr. Thomas Smith who has for several years used Labrador retrievers in his work with seals.* (Kathy Frost)

hunter at the hole or disturb the hole so that the seal would not use it. Then the Native would wait with spear ready at the chosen hole and kill the seal when it surfaced to breathe.

According to Kathy Frost, another ADF&G biologist, Clyde and Charlie, a fellow seal dog, are also adept at finding polar bear tracks, fox scat, bird feathers and their handlers' old lunch spots. When not running a line in search of seal holes, the dogs ride in kennels on sleds pulled by snow machines. As skilled at riding snow machines as he is at finding seal holes, Clyde sometimes rides up front on the snow machine. "Clyde even knows how to lean into the corners," says Frost.

# Last Days of the Tahltan Bear Dog

*By Leslie Kopas*

**Editor's note:** *The following is excerpted from an article which appeared in the June 1982 issue of ALASKA® magazine.*

Other than the breeds used by Eskimos, the Tahltan bear dog is the only aboriginal dog of northern North America still alive. Only six individuals remain, and in as many years — perhaps a little longer — the breed will be extinct. [**Editor's note:** The number of Tahltan bear dogs alive in 1987 is unknown.]

The first white man to note the Tahltan bear dog was the explorer Samuel Black. In 1824, at the headwaters of the Stikine River, he came upon a band of Sekani Indians who had small hunting dogs. He wrote in his diary:

> The Thecannies [Indians] have the art of teaching their small Indian Dogs with erect Ears to hunt alone and the hairy little Beagles will sometimes go a great distance by themselves and tease the animal they fall in with by their constant barking until their master comes up.

The black and white dogs were only 12 to 16 inches at the shoulder and weighed 10 to 18 pounds, yet they were particularly suited for hunting black bears. Their nimbleness, darting attacks and incessant barking brought bears to a baffled standstill. It gave hunters a chance to creep close with bows and arrows for telling shots.

Sometimes Tahltan bear dogs were carried in a sack on the hunter's back to conserve their strength until game was sighted. Unlike sled dogs and pack dogs, they were always well-fed and never ill-treated.

The Tlingit, Casca and Tahltan Indians, as well as the Sekani, raised the small hunting dogs. The Tahltans called the breed "our dog" so it took their name.

The bear dogs were all-around hunting dogs. John Carlick, a Tahltan Indian elder, told me a few years ago:

> They were very smart dogs. They could find a bear's den through deep snow. They could chase up grouse and ptarmigan. They could find rabbits, anything. If you had a bear dog, you could find game; if you didn't have a bear dog, you starved. In the old days they kept the Indians alive.

The invention of the high-powered rifle lessened the value of the dogs, and their numbers began to decline. The first prediction of their demise came in 1906 from ethnologist James Teit. In an ethnography of the Tahltan Indians, he reported:

> . . . A very small variety of native dog generally known as the Tahltan bear dog because it is said they were particularly used in hunting bear. . . . A very few remain, perhaps not more than two or three. . . . This specially small dog of the Tahltan will probably become extinct.

But in 1928, more than 20 years later, Fenley Hunter of New York spent a summer in the Cassiar district of northern British Columbia and reported that two or three bear dogs still survived. And nearly a decade after that, in 1937, Diamond Jenness, an anthropologist at the National Museum of Canada, wrote that "It seems safe to conclude that on the Stikine River we still have a few surviving representatives of an aboriginal American dog."

All the while, Tahltan bear dogs were being shipped out of the North, mostly

*Nancy Dill, among the last of the Tahltan bear dogs, died in 1979. Mrs. June Klein of Carcross, Yukon Territory, owned the little female.* (Courtesy of Leslie Kopas)

by big game outfitter J. Frank Callbreath of Telegraph Creek, whose clients fell in love with the little hunting dogs. As early as 1904, Guy Lawrence, a lineman on the Yukon Telegraph Line, wrote in his diary that the Indians sold bear dogs to big game hunters for $100 each — when they could be persuaded to sell them at all. Several dogs were sent to New York and were dead within a year, supposedly because of the damp climate. (The same fate invariably overtook bear dogs brought to the Alaska coast by Tlingit Indians.) In 1931, dentist Leo P. Bott Jr. took a bear dog from Telegraph Creek to Little Rock, Arkansas. When the animal died a few months later, the dentist hired a taxidermist to mount the skin, which he presented to the National Museum of Canada.

While posted at Telegraph Creek, Constable J. Blakiston-Gray of the British Columbia Provincial Police acquired 10 bear dogs as pets between 1936 and 1940. When he was assigned to Lytton in southern British Columbia, he took five of them with him. He persuaded the Canadian Kennel Club to recognize the Tahltan bear dog as a registered breed. Shortly afterward, the Provincial Police Inspector paid a visit and was flabbergasted to find the oldest police office, jail and gallows in the province occupied by Tahltan bear dogs.

Blakiston-Gray's days as a dog breeder were over. He gave his animals to Harriet Morgan, who registered three more with the Canadian Kennel Club in 1944 and one more in 1948. She hoped to breed Tahltan bear dogs on a commercial scale in Windsor, Ontario.

Harriet Morgan's kennel business was not successful, and she moved to California. No more Tahltan bear dogs were registered with the Canadian Kennel Club.

In 1966, Edward Hoagland, a New York writer, visited Telegraph Creek gathering material for his book, *Notes from the Century Before.* In the book he wrote:

The bear dogs! What are there, two or three left? Long before the grizzlies are exterminated, the last Tahltan bear dog will be dead. One wants to record them for the future — that they were black and pint-sized, vociferous, skinny, gutsy, that they moved on springs, lived by their wits, darted about, apprehensive as well as courageous, and that they seemed to know in these final few years that they were doomed as a race.

Had an effort been made in 1969, the breed might still have been rescued. At that time, Tahltan bear dogs lived at Telegraph Creek, Iskut and Atlin in British Columbia, and at Whitehorse, Carcross and Keno in Yukon. Yet . . . the owners were spaying nearly all the females.

In 1975, I arrived in the North with Edward Hoagland's book in hand. I was not a dog fancier. In fact, I had never owned anything but a mutt. . . . Nonetheless, the idea of seeing a native dog intrigued me. I inquired at Telegraph Creek. I was told I was six years too late.

A few days later, from a chance remark at Carcross, Yukon, I picked up the trail of the bear dog again. Making something of a nuisance of myself, I knocked on doors across southern Yukon and northern British Columbia. Mostly I heard stories about bear dogs that had died recently. But I also found 11 living Tahltan bear dogs: three at Carcross, two at Whitehorse and six at Atlin. Except for one, the animals were males or spayed females. The unspayed female died a few months later without giving birth.

The owners of the dogs were somewhat chagrined to hear that the Tahltan bear dog was virtually extinct. They had assumed that there were still many bear dogs "somewhere else" in the North, and perhaps even outside it.

# From Niki With Love

John Madden, a self-described Renaissance man, is in fact a man of many interests and talents. Originally from Texas, this four-year Alaskan is a budget officer for the National Weather Service. When not at work, Madden spends his time with Niki, his 6-year-old Samoyed. Constant companions, Madden and Niki are outdoors hiking and camping year-round, and are often involved in community projects.

Niki also figures prominently in one of Madden's favorite hobbies, spinning and knitting. Niki provides the fleece, Madden the talent and creativity needed to transform the fleece into scarves, mittens and ear warmers. Madden's interest in spinning began about five years ago when he decided Niki's combed and shed hair should be put to some use. Naturally talented when it comes to needlework, Madden quickly came upon the idea of spinning the hair into yarn and knitting it.

He uses a steel comb to remove the fleece (the undercoat), which is then

LEFT: *This handful of fleece, weighing about 16 ounces, is the result of one year of combing Niki.* (Laurie Thompson, staff)

ABOVE: *Madden demonstrates the drop spindle, the first mechanical device developed for spinning fleece into yarn.* (Laurie Thompson, staff)

*Using a traditional spinning wheel, Madden spins Niki's fleece into yarn. Approximately 10 hours of spinning yields enough yarn for a pair of mittens.* (Laurie Thompson, staff)

spun by handfuls into yarn. In addition to a traditional spinning wheel, Madden occasionally uses a drop spindle, a round stick with tapered ends, the first device invented to aid in hand spinning. After enough fleece is spun, the knitting begins.

Most Samoyeds will yield approximately 16 ounces of good quality, off-white fleece per year, which can be made into enough yarn to make four pairs of three-ply mittens or one

scarf, two pairs of mittens and a cap. Surprisingly, these garments can be washed in hot water and machine-dried; repeated washing raises a nap similar to angora. It takes Madden 10 hours of spinning time and 10 hours of knitting with double-pointed needles to produce a pair of mittens which are lighter in weight than wool and which keep his hands warm and dry at minus 25 degrees.

Since the fleece is not cut or sheared as with sheep, but rather combed off, the hair has no blunt edges which might make the knitted garment scratchy and uncomfortable to wear. The only exception to this is when Madden may add a few outer guard hairs to mittens for strength. The yarn also seems to be

*This scarf with a twist, one of Madden's designs, can be secured around the neck by inserting one end through a loop in the opposite end.* (Laurie Thompson, staff)

hypoallergenic and can be worn by those who suffer from allergies to dogs.

Madden confines the giving of his articles to relatives and special friends, but the real enjoyment comes from producing the garments. He has found that some people are surprised at the idea of a dog hair product, but become more accepting once they realize nothing has happened to the dog but a bit of grooming.

*Products made and modeled by Madden from Samoyed fleece are an ear warmer, mittens and muffler. The mittens have kept Madden's hands warm at minus-25 degrees.* (Laurie Thompson, staff)

# Racing Dogs

What bull-fighting is to the Spaniard, horse racing to the Kentuckian, a marathon to the Greek, Derby Day to the Englishman, so is the annual All Alaska Sweepstakes to the Alaskan.

Esther Birdsall Darling,
*The Great Dog Races of Nome*
(1916)

## The Early Years

Until the early 1900s, mushers and sled dogs had maintained a strict working relationship. There was little time for fun or games when drivers harnessed their teams.

Certainly there were occasions when sled dogs were raced, perhaps to settle a bet or determine the fastest team in the neighborhood, camp or village. But there had never been a major organized mushing event, complete with official rules, judges, trail and purse, until 1908, when a group of sled dog owners in Nome staged the "first great race" — the All Alaska Sweepstakes.

And although the sweepstakes dominated the early days of sled dog racing in Alaska, numerous smaller-scale and usually short-lived mushing events started up around the territory before World War I.

In Nome, other notable races staged during the sweepstakes years included the Solomon Derby, Borden Cup Marathon and Joy Race.

The Solomon Derby was held in February or March and was considered

*One of the more notable early-day sled dog races was the Solomon Derby, a 65-mile event considered a warmup for the longer All Alaska Sweepstakes. Shown here is the team owned by Scotty Allan and Esther Birdsall Darling, driven by Percy Blatchford, lining up for the start of the 1914 Derby.*
(The Anchorage Museum)

...ERA HOME ALASKA, MARCH 2ⁿᵈ 1914
...T OF ALLANS DARLING ENTRY, PERCY BLATCHFORD, DRIVER

**FIRST DOG RACE — OLD KNIK AND RETURN**
**ANCHORAGE KENNEL CLUB**

| LEAVE OUT | DOGS | ENTRIES | DRIVER | NO | A.M. | P.M. | P.M. | TIME (WEATHER) |
|---|---|---|---|---|---|---|---|---|
| 9:10 | 6 | MATHEWSON / BOWKER | GREER | 2 | BUNCHED 3 AND 4 POSITION | 12:25 / 12:27½ | 1:20¼ / 1:41 | WEATHER BAD 10 BELOW Z |
| 9:00 | 5 | GUSTUFSON | SELF | 1 | | 12:25 / 12:29½ | 1:21 / 1:41 | HEAVY NORTH WIND |
| 9:20 | 7 | HOWARD | SELF | 3 | SECOND 11:28 | 12:25 / 12:29 | 1:15½ / 1:18 | TRAIL HEAVY |
| | | REVELL | | | | | | |
| 9:30 A.M. | 5 | DIXON | SELF | 4 | FIRST 11:28 | 12:14½ | 1:09½ / 1:30 | SNOW DRIFTING BAD |

| ANCHORAGE | JANUARY 20 1916 | | | | EAGLE RIVER 14 M. | BOARDING CARS 17½ M. | PETERS CREEK 23 M. | OLD KNIK 27 M. | TOTAL TIME |
|---|---|---|---|---|---|---|---|---|---|
| P.M. | | MATHEWSON | | | | | | P.M. | H M |
| 5:50 | 6 | BOWKER | GREER | 2 | 4:38 | 3:31 | 2:30 | 1:41 | 8:40 |
| 6:00:30 | 5 | GUSTUFSON | SELF | 1 | 4:38 | 3:31 | 2:30 | 1:41 | 9:00:30 |
| 5:19 | 7 | HOWARD | SELF | 3 | 3:48 | 2:52 | 2:02 | 1:18 | 7:59 |
| OUT | | REVELL | | | | | | | |
| 5:22 | 5 | DIXON | SELF | 4 | 4:02 | 3:00 | 2:10½ / 2:11 | 1:30 | 7:52 |

McCAIN STUDIO

*A sign tells the story of Anchorage's first official dog race, organized by the Anchorage Kennel Club and run on January 20, 1916. The race, 54 miles to Old Knik and back, was won by Frank Dixon and his five-dog team.*
(The Anchorage Museum)

second in importance to the sweepstakes. The 65-mile event went from Nome to Solomon and back and was considered a warm-up for the 408-mile sweepstakes, as well as a good measure of a team's speed.

The Borden Cup Marathon, which covered a distance of 26⅓ miles, lasted 16 years. The record time of 1 hour, 55 minutes and 20 seconds was set by Leonhard Seppala, who won the race four times.

The Joy Race, officially named the Kamoogen Handicap Burden Race, was a fun race, a celebration of spring. The entrants drove teams 75 miles from Nome to Council. The handicap burden of each musher was the lady of his choice.

Along the Yukon River, the village of Ruby also developed a kennel club. From 1913 to 1916, the club staged the Ruby Dog Derby, run over a 58-mile course to Long City and back.

Other historic races were recorded at Iditarod and even Anchorage. The first annual Iditarod Sweepstakes Race was staged on New Year's Day, 1911. Claude Shea, driving a five-dog team, won the 20-mile race and took the $350 prize.

The Anchorage Kennel Club organized Anchorage's first race in January 1916. The 54-mile race started in front of the Crest Hotel, on Fourth Avenue in downtown Anchorage, and went to Knik and back.

Beginning in 1918 sled dog racing in Alaska went through a decade-long lull. When serious, organized racing resumed in 1927, the sport had a new center of interest: Fairbanks.

Three events began in 1927 and 1928 — the Signal Corps Race, the H. Wendell Endicott Trophy Race and the Fromm Trophy Ladies Race. The races lasted into the mid-1930s, and served as forerunners for the Fairbanks Sweepstakes Race and, ultimately, the North American Championship Sled Dog Race, one of Alaska's most prestigious mushing events.

The three events also marked a new trend in sled dog racing, emphasizing small, fast dogs. Mushers and owners worked to improve breeding and feeding practices and developed new training procedures. Races became shorter and faster. Eventually a system of heats was devised in which races were run over short courses on two or three successive days, with the winner determined by total time.

The Endicott Trophy Race was a short sprint, at first 17¼ miles long and eventually shortened to 16 miles. It called for dogs of lightning speed. A trio of Natives from the lower Yukon River, Fred and Joe Stickman of Nulato and Walter Nollner of Galena, dominated the race from 1928 to 1930. Musher and trapper Bob Buzby won the final event and retired the trophy in 1933.

The Signal Corps Trophy was created and sponsored by the Washington to Alaska Military Cable and Telegraph System; the trophy was to be given to the first driver to win the race three times. That feat was not accomplished until 1935, when Bob Buzby claimed the trophy. The Signal Corps Race initially went from Fairbanks to Summit (near Chatanika) and back, over a difficult, mountainous 58-mile course. In 1931, its format was changed to

**ABOVE:** *Mrs. Currin drives her team in the First Ladies' Dog Race of Alaska, held in the Iditarod mining district on January 14, 1914. The 20.2-mile course ran from Flat to Discovery and back, then on to Iditarod and back to Flat. Mrs. Currin finished fourth.*
(Courtesy of Earl Norris)

**BELOW:** *Whipping down the spectator-lined main street of Anchorage is Mrs. Casy Jones, leading in the 1916 Ladies Dogteam Race.* (The Anchorage Museum)

LEFT: *Mushers gather to draw for starting positions in a 1930s race in Fairbanks. Included in the group are some of the top racers of the period: Bob Buzby (standing, extreme left); Johnny Allen (signing in); Mike Agbaba (standing at Allen's left elbow); and Leonhard Seppala (peering over Allen's shoulder).* (Revel Griffin Collection, University of Alaska Archives, Fairbanks)

RIGHT: *Leonhard Seppala drives his team along a Fairbanks street during the 1946 Winter Ice Carnival. Seppala, best known for his part in the 1925 diphtheria serum run to Nome, lived in Fairbanks from 1928 until he retired from mushing and moved to Seattle in the 1950s. He died in 1967 at 90.* (Jim Brown, © 1946)

two 30-mile heats on successive days, and in 1935 the course was altered again to run 80 miles from Fairbanks to Salcha and back.

The Fromm Trophy Ladies Race, run on a course identical to that of the Endicott race, paved the way for modern women's sled dog events. From 1927 to 1929 two sisters, Genevieve and Hortense Parker of Fairbanks, captured attention by combining for three firsts and a second. The race was discontinued in 1932 and 1933,

resumed in 1934, and ended for good in 1935.

In 1936, the Signal Corps Race gave way to the Fairbanks Sweepstakes, a three-day, 90-mile event. That same year, an Indian musher from the lower Yukon River, Johnny Allen, began his reign as the Interior's fastest sled dog driver. Allen, who cross-bred Irish setters with native dogs and wolves, swept the Fairbanks Sweepstakes from 1936 to 1938.

The sweepstakes race was lengthened

and toughened in 1940. A 165-mile course was laid out from Fairbanks to Livengood and back. Much of the route passed through mountainous terrain and the sweepstakes earned a reputation as the "toughest in all Fairbanks racing history." This was also the first year that racing was carried by radio throughout the Territory.

World War II effectively stopped all organized competitive mushing in Alaska from 1942 until 1946, bringing to an end another era of sled dog racing.

# All Alaska Sweepstakes

The All Alaska Sweepstakes sled dog race was the brainchild of the Nome Kennel Club, organized in 1907 to "make sled dog racing a recognized part of the life of the community." The first sweepstakes, run in April 1908, was truly a big event for Nome, described as having "all the pomp and ceremony of carnival time in sunny lands." Schools and courts adjourned on race day and most businesses closed. John Hegness won the race, driving a team owned by Albert Fink, president of the kennel club.

As part of the race festivities, a queen and maids of honor were elected. Each of those who voted was charged 1 cent; the money raised became part of the race purse.

The race started and finished at Barracks Square on Front Street. The Board of Trade Saloon served as race headquarters. It was there that "the people crowded to read the news on the blackboard and place their bets."

The winners' purse varied from year to year, depending on the state of the local economy. The first year, the prize was $10,000.

The 408-mile course from Nome to Candle and back followed a telegraph line, so messages from houses, camps and villages along the trail were continuously

*Driving a team owned by Nome Kennel Club president Albert Fink, John Hegness took first place and a $10,000 prize in the inaugural All Alaska Sweepstakes in Nome in 1908.* (Lomen Brothers, courtesy of the Iditarod Trail Committee)

sent back to Nome. Bulletins with updates on the race leaders and the condition of men and dogs were posted throughout town.

To guarantee that the contestants would take good care of their dogs and follow a code of fair play, the Nome Kennel Club instituted a set of race rules, many of which are still in effect in races across Alaska, Canada and the Lower 48. The rules encouraged good treatment of dogs along

**BELOW:** *Esther Birdsall Darling, member of the Nome Kennel Club and partner with musher Scotty Allan, stands with two of her dogs, Kid and Baldy. Baldy (on the right) led Allan's team for several successful years and was immortalized in Darling's book, "Baldy of Nome."* (Courtesy of Earl Norris)

**RIGHT:** *Scotty Allan poses with the team he drove to victory in the 4th All Alaska Sweepstakes in Nome in 1911. Allan's partner and co-owner of the dogs was writer Esther Birdsall Darling. Allan-Darling teams took two firsts, two seconds and two third places in the six sweepstakes they entered.* (Carrie McLain Museum)

*Kolyma (left), shown with owner John "Iron Man" Johnson and teammate Jolte, gained fame as the best dog ever to run in the All Alaska Sweepstakes.* (Courtesy of Earl Norris)

*In Nome, spectators line the street and watch from balconies and reviewing stands as L. Coke Hill's team starts the 4th Annual All Alaska Sweepstakes in 1911. Hill's team covered the 408-mile course in 81 hours, taking second place.* (The Anchorage Museum)

the trail. To ensure that no driver would attempt to make illegal substitutions during the race, each dog was photographed and its name, color and markings were recorded in the club's books.

The sleds the mushers used were typically made of hickory and lashed together with reindeer sinew or walrus hide. The mushers carried an assortment of furs plus "water boots" for themselves and blankets, flannel booties and eye "veils" (for protection in strong sunlight) for the dogs.

Hegness won the inaugural sweepstakes driving a mail-dog team, complete with freighting harness and sled. The winner of the second sweepstakes, Scotty Allan, used a sleeker, lighter sled weighing only 31 pounds, and new and simpler harnesses, which allowed the dogs greater freedom of movement. Modern racing sleds are generally patterned after that model. Some of the designs were borrowed from styles Natives used before the days of Alaska's gold rush.

In the 1909 race, a team driven by Norwegian immigrant Louis Thrustrup and owned by a Russian fur trader named William Goosak earned the greatest attention. Thrustrup ran Siberian huskies, much

*Musher Scotty Allan poses with his leader, Baldy. The dog was bred for freight work, but later proved himself to be a champion racer, competing in all 10 All Alaska Sweepstakes races.* (Alaska Northwest Publishing)

smaller and lighter than the big, powerful freighting dog breeds used by the majority of the contestants.

Fox Maule Ramsay, a Scottish miner and sportsman, liked the qualities of the dogs so much that he traveled to Siberia the following summer and purchased several of the small huskies. Ramsay brought the dogs back to Nome, accompanied by two Russian handlers.

In 1910, Ramsay entered three teams of Siberians in the sweepstakes. One of the teams was driven by John "Iron Man" Johnson, who won the event in 74 hours,

14 minutes and 37 seconds, a record that was never broken. Ramsay, driving his own team of Siberians, finished second.

The Alaskan dogs, meanwhile, included malamutes or other native Alaskan huskies, setters, pointers, collies, hounds, Airedales or breeds mixed with huskies.

The final years of the sweepstakes saw a drop-off in the field of entrants; in 1917, the final year, only four teams entered. According to Esther Birdsall Darling, the sweepstakes races were discontinued because of World War I.

Leonhard Seppala, who had won the

*Musher Faye Delzene poses for a photo with his team after their victory in the 1913 All Alaska Sweepstakes race.* (Lomen Brothers, courtesy of the Iditarod Trail Committee)

race in 1915, 1916 and 1917, observed, "Whether the war had anything to do with the cessation of the All Alaska Sweepstakes, or whether there were no teams suitable for competition, I do not know. However, I doubt there will ever be a dog race instituted which will so test the mettle of dogs and driver as did the All Alaska Sweepstakes."

A blackboard in the Board of Trade Saloon in Nome keeps race enthusiasts informed of the standings of All Alaska Sweepstakes entrants. The race course followed the telegraph line so that progress reports could be sent back to Nome regularly during the event. (The Anchorage Museum)

# Seventy-Five Years Later

The ghosts of Alaska's early sled dog racing glory days were awakened in late March 1983, when nearly two dozen mushers gathered in Nome for the 75th anniversary running of the All Alaska Sweepstakes. The 23 drivers who entered the 408-mile event pursued more than the $25,000 winner-take-all purse, they chased the memories of Alaska's earliest mushing legends.

The special diamond anniversary race was staged by the Nome Kennel Club to commemorate the first race, run in 1908. Like the original, the 1983 race

*Running in second place in the 1983 75th anniversary running of the All Alaska Sweepstakes race, Rick Swenson drives his team out of Council. Swenson won the race in 84 hours, 42 minutes and four seconds.* (J. Schultz)

*The crowd forms a chute for starting teams at the 75th anniversary All Alaska Sweepstakes race, staged by the Nome Kennel Club in 1983.* (J. Schultz)

followed a route from Nome to Candle and back. And like the earlier sweepstakes series, the anniversary event required mushers to finish with all the dogs with which they started and no others.

Rick Swenson of Eureka, best known for his Iditarod victories, reached the finish line in 84 hours and 42 minutes. The winning time was only the sixth fastest in sweepstakes history and nearly 10 hours slower than the record set in 1910, when Iron Man Johnson's team ran the course in 74 hours, 14 minutes and 37 seconds.

*Musher Rick Swenson, windburned and beaming, talks with reporters and race fans in Nome following his first-place finish in the 75th anniversary running of the All Alaska Sweepstakes in April 1983.* (J. Schultz)

*Musher Jerry Austin nears the Haven
checkpoint during the 1983 anniversary
running of the All Alaska Sweepstakes.*
(J. Schultz)

# Dog Mushing Today

Sled dog racing today is a booming sport, with more events, more mushers and more sled dogs than ever before.

Racing begins throughout the North in November and ends in April. For a musher willing to travel, there are races nearly every weekend during the winter.

Although open-class (no limit on number of dogs) sprint races, such as the Fur Rendezvous World Championship and the North American Championship, and middle- to long-distance events, such as the Kusko 300, Coldfoot Classic, Iditarod and Yukon Quest, get most of the publicity, by far the largest number of mushers compete in the shorter, smaller, limited-class races.

Limited-class events — anything from three- to eight-dog races — are popular throughout the North, from Anchorage to Tok to Whitehorse to arctic villages. These races are perfect for mushers who can't afford big kennels or the full-time commitment needed for open-class sprints and long-distance treks.

*A musher gingerly leads his team through 30-mph winds to cross frozen Ernie Creek during the 1984 Coldfoot Classic race. The race runs 350 miles through the Brooks Range, from Coldfoot to Anaktuvuk Pass, then to Bettles and back to Coldfoot.* (Pete Bowers)

The quality of limited-class dogs is as good as that of open-class sprint teams, and there certainly is no lack of competition. Some of the state's premier open-class mushers — Roxy Wright, George Attla, Joee Redington Jr., Marvin Kokrine and Kathy Frost — also run limited-class events. Often, open-class mushers will use limited-class races to give their young dogs race experience in a lower-pressure setting.

Expansion has also hit the open-class sprints. The Fur Rendezvous World Championship and the North American are the top two in prestige among Alaska's top

*Although most attention is focused on Alaska's major sled dog races — such as the Iditarod, World Championship and North American Championship — smaller races are held in communities throughout the state. Here, an unidentified musher drives his team in the 1983 Copper River Classic Sled Dog Race.* (Ken Roberson)

sprints. But the status of the other two members of the "big four" sprint races, the Alaska State Championship and Tok Race of Champions, has been challenged by several other open-class events.

Another growing race category is the middle-distance event, which includes 90- to 350-mile races. Such races were virtually nonexistent from after World War II until the 1970s. By 1985, there were numerous middle-distance events, such as the Coldfoot Classic.

The Iditarod is responsible for the large increase of middle-distance events. In 1983, Iditarod organizers added a rookie qualification rule that requires all rookies to complete an approved 200-mile-or-longer race before being eligible to compete in the Iditarod.

Also popular are races for junior mushers. Nearly all mushing clubs and associations offer events for younger drivers. The first Junior North American races were held in Fairbanks in the early 1950s. A Junior World Championship has been staged during Fur Rendezvous for more than two decades. Since 1978, there has even been a Junior Iditarod, which began as a 50-mile event, expanding to 130 miles in 1981.

**UPPER LEFT:** *Musher Susan Butcher crosses the ice of Norton Bay near the end of the 1986 Iditarod Trail Sled Dog Race.* (Al Grillo)

**LEFT:** *Trail guards work to put a tangled team back into order. Tangled teams are only one of the many hazards a musher may encounter along the race trail.*
(Third Eye Photography)

LEFT: *Kathy Redington rounds a bend on the 12-mile Women's World Championship Sled Dog Race course in 1985. Redington placed third in the three-day event.* (Jane Gnass)

BELOW: *Joee Redington Jr. stops for a nap along the trail at Candle during the 75th anniversary All Alaska Sweepstakes race in 1983.* (J. Schultz)

*Sled dogs wait in their dog box, on the back
of a pickup truck, to be harnessed up for
Don's Iditarod 200 race in Willow in 1985.*
(Bill Sherwonit)

Harnessed and bootied, two sled dogs await the start of a race. (J. Schultz)

ABOVE: *The best known Outsider to compete in Alaskan sled dog races is Dr. Roland Lombard, a veterinarian from Wayland, Massachusetts. During his peak years, Lombard won 26 championship races throughout the state. Here, Lombard drives his team in the 1984 Fur Rendezvous World Championship Sled Dog Race, an event he has won eight times.* (Jane Gnass)

LEFT: *Young Mike Holland holds on tight during a children's one-dog race in Happy Valley, near Homer, in 1982.* (Chlaus Lotscher)

*Jake Butler of Tanana, winner of the first Fur Rendezvous dog race, poses with his team. The race, held in 1946, ran 17.6 miles from Sixth Avenue and F Street to Campbell Airstrip and back. Butler's three-day total elapsed time was four hours, 17 minutes and 37 seconds.* (Robinson Studios, courtesy of Earl Norris)

# Major Races

## Anchorage's Fur Rendezvous

The post-war 1940s were critical to the development of sled dog racing in Alaska. In Fairbanks, the North American championships succeeded the sweepstakes races

of the late 1930s and early 1940s. And in Anchorage, the Fur Rendezvous Sled Dog Race was born.

During the last four decades, the Fur Rondy race has grown to world championship status, earning a reputation as one of the two premier sprint races in Alaska. But the Rondy's origins were not nearly so grand. The inaugural Fur Rendezvous Sled Dog Race, organized in 1946 by Earl Norris of Anchorage, Jake Butler of Tanana and Sgt. Clint Thurman of Fort Richardson, was only an exhibition and was accompanied by little hoopla, little publicity and little money. The total purse was a meager $175.

The first race followed a 17.6-mile course from Sixth Avenue and F Street to Campbell Airstrip and back. Interest was sufficiently high to make the race an annual event. Gradually it grew from a Fur Rendezvous sideshow into the midwinter festival's premier attraction, attended by thousands of spectators. The race also grew in size, status and acclaim within the mushing community.

In 1948 the starting line was shifted and the official race distance was lengthened to 25 miles, a standard that has remained to the present. (The exact distance varies from year to year, depending on weather and trail conditions. In 1986, for the first time in its history, the race was cancelled because of lack of snow.)

In 1951 the Rondy event was named the All-Alaska Sled Dog Race, and the purse

**ABOVE:** *Musher Dick Mitchell takes off down Fourth Avenue in this mid-1950s Alaska Championship Sled Dog Race. The race, held during Anchorage's Fur Rendezvous, later became known as the World Championship Sled Dog Race.*
(Alaska Northwest Publishing)

**RIGHT:** *Anchorage's Fur Rendezvous offers more than races for dog lovers. Each year, crowds gather to watch the strongest dogs compete in the Weight Pulling Contest. Here, Kelly Wilson tries to persuade Taz to pull a sled laden with concrete weights.*
(Third Eye Photography)

had risen to $6,000. Two other name and status changes followed: in 1953, the event became the Alaska Championship Sled Dog Race; then, in 1961, it graduated to billing as the World Championship Sled Dog Race.

As the race's status increased, so did its monetary award — the 1985 race offered a record $50,000 purse. In 1987, the next year the race was run, Eddy Streeper took his first-place prize from a smaller purse of $30,000, as did 1988 winner Charlie Champaine.

Literally thousands of mushing fans, tourists and just-plain-curious folks line the streets and trails of Anchorage for a look at some of the best mushers and sled dog teams in the world.

Race day in downtown Anchorage is bedlam. Fourth Avenue — covered by snow which has been trucked in and laid down prior to the start — is a cacophony of yips, howls, barks and growls as it is taken over by two dozen mushers and a couple of hundred dogs.

The teams depart at two-minute intervals. Most of the race course is located within the city limits and presents numerous challenges. There are enough steep hills, hairpin turns and road crossings to be navigated that at least one musher has referred to the Rondy as a steeplechase event.

Each year there are mishaps of some sort: a bewildered leader will head into the crowd; a musher will lose control of his dogs; a team will bolt and run away from

its driver; or teams will become hopelessly entangled trying to pass one another.

The obstacles, natural or otherwise, and the 25-mile distance create an ultimate challenge for mushers and dogs, one that tests stamina, endurance and discipline as well as speed.

"It's not just a test of speed," says veteran Anchorage musher Jim Welch. "The fastest team doesn't always win. The best team wins."

**ABOVE:** *Roxy Wright, following in the footsteps of parents Vera and Gareth Wright, rounds a bend on the trail of the World Championship Sled Dog Race in Anchorage in 1983. Through 1985, Wright had won eight championship titles.* (Ron Wendt)

**RIGHT:** *Charlie Champaine of Salcha runs along with his team toward the Fourth Avenue finish line of the 1984 World Championship Sled Dog Race in Anchorage. Champaine won the three-day event with a total elapsed time of 254 minutes, four seconds.* (Third Eye Photography)

*Veteran mushers George Attla (left) and Charlie Champaine pass the time before the start of the 1984 Fur Rendezvous World Championship Sled Dog Race in Anchorage.* (Jane Gnass)

# George Attla

George Attla is probably the most famous native Alaskan musher ever to race a team of dogs. Many would argue that the Athabascan Indian is the best sled dog racer, ever.

When Dr. Roland Lombard, a legend within Alaska's dog-mushing circles, was asked in 1982 to name the number-one sled dog racer, Lombard replied with a smile, "I think you can go by the numbers."

And by the numbers, Attla is far and away Alaska's all-time best. In a racing career that has spanned more than a quarter of a century, Attla has won dozens of races, both big and small.

Attla's credits include wins in the Rondy, North American, Alaska State Championship, Tok Race of Champions and many smaller races.

Yet numbers alone don't come close to telling the Attla story. His is a saga of tragedy, heroism and pride.

Attla was born in 1933 in Alaska's Interior and grew up in the Athabascan village of Huslia. Like most villagers in the Alaskan Bush during the first half of the 20th century, Attla grew up around sled dogs.

Mushing dogs was a way of life. Almost from the time he could walk, Attla helped his father run a team of dogs along the family trap line. That boyhood friendship with dogs was interrupted at age 8 when Attla contracted tuberculosis. But he was lucky; by the early 1940s, the Public

ABOVE: *George Attla, Alaska's most famous native musher, draws a number to determine his starting position in the 1982 World Championship Sled Dog Race.* (Staff)

RIGHT: *Amid lightly falling snow, George Attla checks his team (still in their dog box) prior to the start of the 1981 World Championship Sled Dog Race in Anchorage.*
(Chlaus Lotscher)

Health Service had discovered ways to fight the disease.

Attla began a long series of hospital stays. The tuberculosis had affected his knee, requiring a bone fusion which permanently locked the knee joint. Attla could walk, but with a limp.

He spent most of the next decade undergoing treatment in Tanana and at Mount Edgecumbe Hospital near Sitka, then he returned to Huslia. He'd been cured, but scars, both physical and mental, remained.

Then Attla rediscovered his love — he took up mushing again. At first, he competed only in local races. But after earning a reputation as one of Huslia's top mushers, he wanted more. Finally, in 1958, as a 24-year-old rookie, George represented Huslia in Anchorage's Fur Rendezvous race.

Perhaps Attla's greatest attribute is his dedication to the sport. After a quarter of a century of racing, Attla's dedication has paid large dividends. Despite the fused kneecap, despite glaucoma that has caused him to lose sight in his right eye, despite the loss of a finger due to an injury suffered during a training run, he remains, in his 50s, the musher to beat.

And now the silver-haired, stiff-legged musher is also an overwhelming favorite with the crowds. He's easily the most recognized figure in any sprint race.

*As his team stretches out before him, George Attla seems to relax behind his sled in the 1982 North American Championship Sled Dog Race in Fairbanks.* (Staff)

*Roger Nordlum of Kotzebue leaves the*
*downtown Anchorage starting line of the*
*1985 Iditarod Trail Sled Dog Race.*
(Bill Sherwonit)

## The Last Great Race

During winter 1966 an Alaskan history buff and an outdoorsman with wanderlust had a conversation which forever changed the sport of dog mushing in Alaska.

Wanderer Joe Redington Sr. was born in Oklahoma and spent most of his youth traveling back and forth across the United States with his father James and brother Ray. The Redington clan moved to Alaska in 1948. That same year, Joe started up his Knik Kennels and began using sled dogs to make a living.

History buff Dorothy Page saw her first sled dog race in 1960, shortly after moving to Alaska from New Mexico. In 1966, Page was named chairman of the Wasilla-Knik Centennial Committee. Her job was to find an event to celebrate the 100th anniversary of America's purchase of Alaska from Russia in 1867.

"We decided to have a spectacular sled dog race to wake Alaskans up to what mushers had done for Alaska. We wanted to pay a tribute to the mushers; they opened up the state and were the sole means of winter transportation for years," she later explained.

A race along the Iditarod Trail came to mind for two reasons. It was a famous route used by mushers to bring supplies, passengers, mail and food to many Alaskan communities during the gold rush days; and it passed through Knik, which would bring the race close to home.

Despite opposition to the idea of a centennial race, the first Iditarod was a smashing success. The two-day, 56-mile race attracted a field of 58 of the world's best mushers and offered a $25,000 purse — by far the biggest payoff in mushing up to that time.

But the Iditarod appeared to be a one-time event. The race was cancelled in 1968

*Signs and fluorescent pink tape mark the Iditarod Trail for race entrants. In bad weather, mushers occasionally lose the trail despite the markers.* (Chlaus Lotscher)

*A carefully packed sled, containing equipment and cold weather gear for the Iditarod Trail, stands ready for its musher. Essential is a large supply of booties to protect the dogs' feet.* (Both by Jane Gnass)

**ABOVE:** *Race veterinarian Ed Wendt prepares vitamin B complex for a dog. Dog care along the trail has increased since volunteer veterinarians have been stationed at checkpoints.* (J. Schultz)

**RIGHT:** *Musher Susan Butcher takes off through the crowd at the Settlers Bay restart of the 1985 Iditarod Trail Sled Dog Race.* (J. Schultz)

*Susan Butcher and her lead dog pose on Front Street in Nome following their first-place finish in the 1986 Iditarod Trail race.* (Al Grillo)

**ABOVE:** *Children in McGrath took a holiday from school when the 1984 Iditarod mushers passed through town. Here, two of the youngsters give some attention to Jerry Austin's team.* (AP Laserphoto; courtesy of the *Anchorage Times*)

**RIGHT:** *Musher Sue Firmin adjusts her team at Goose Lake in Anchorage, during the start of the 1983 Iditarod Trail Sled Dog Race.* (Alissa Crandall)

for lack of snow. In 1969, the race was reinstated, but only $1,000 could be raised. Not surprisingly, the field shrank to 12 mushers.

By 1972, Redington and the Iditarod committee had decided to expand the race to make it longer, better and richer. Initially, they planned a race from Knik to the gold-boom ghost town of Iditarod, but changed the finish to Nome. Most members of the mushing community, as well as the media, greeted Redington's thousand-mile dream with skepticism.

Several obstacles had to be overcome. The trail had to be located and cleared, and, to attract mushers, a large purse had to be raised. The Army helped to locate and clear a large portion of the Iditarod Trail, and agreed to help break trail, to test a group of snowmachines.

With a trail and the promise of a $50,000 purse, 34 teams signed up for the 1973 first-ever 1,100-mile Iditarod Trail Sled Dog Race from Anchorage to Nome.

The 1975 Iditarod was a landmark race for two reasons: ARCO became a major sponsor, pledging $50,000; and several rules were added to ensure proper care and health of the dogs.

*Carl Huntington, defending Iditarod champion, stops to rest his dogs during the 1975 race. Huntington, who started with 12 dogs, dropped out of the race at Galena when three of his seven remaining dogs became dehydrated.* (Anchorage Times)

BELOW: *Musher Burt Bomhoff relaxes at Ophir during a break from the 1985 Iditarod Trail Sled Dog Race.* (J. Schultz)

RIGHT: *The mushers aren't the only ones who need to rest at checkpoints during long distance races such as the Iditarod.* (Al Grillo)

RIGHT: *Libby Riddles of Teller, first woman to win the Iditarod Trail Sled Dog Race, poses for the press in Nome following her 1985 victory.* (J. Schultz)

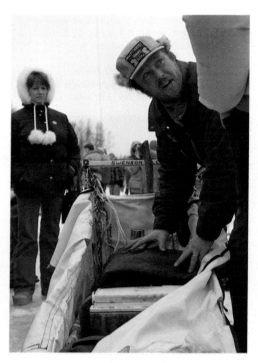

In 1985, Col. Norman Vaughan, 80, competed in the Iditarod Trail Sled Dog Race, the oldest musher ever to enter the race. Unfortunately, Vaughan was injured early in the race and was forced to scratch. (Bill Sherwonit)

Rick Swenson packs his sled before starting the 1982 Iditarod Trail Sled Dog Race. Swenson's mushing career began in 1976; by 1986, he had won four of the 10 Iditarod races he had entered. (Brad W. Ebel)

Herbie Nayokpuk of Shishmaref harnesses one of his dogs in preparation for the restart of the 1981 Iditarod Trail Sled Dog Race at Settlers Bay. (Brad W. Ebel)

The Iditarod finally appeared to have it made. But things got worse again in 1976. Because of negative publicity regarding dog deaths and treatment, ARCO ended its financial backing of the race. Again the Iditarod was left without a major sponsor.

On January 6, 1976, the entire Iditarod Board of Directors quit. Redington took over as president and got Dorothy Page and her husband, Von, to help run the show. The race survived and it has steadily grown in stature since, gaining national and international credibility and fame as "The Last Great Race."

Women have dominated the Iditarod in recent years. In 1985, Libby Riddles of Teller became the first woman to win the race, taking home a $50,000 prize. Once the ground was broken, no one could stop Susan Butcher of Manley, who drove her team to victory in 1986, 1987 and 1988.

After a ceremonial start in downtown Anchorage, the race begins officially in Wasilla. The mushers follow the trail through the Alaska Range, into the Interior and along the Yukon River, through the Kuskokwim Mountains and along the coast of Norton Sound, passing through 27 checkpoints.

Danger is part of the game, whether it's holes in river ice, angry moose blocking the route, unmarked stretches of trail, whiteout conditions, howling winds or minus 50- to 60-degree temperatures that cause frostbitten fingers, feet and faces.

Exhaustion is also an occupational

*Tim Osmar dashes over the finish line in 1984 to win his third Junior Iditarod Sled Dog Race.* (J. Schultz)

*Lance Barve, son of musher Lavon Barve, leads his dogs to the Settlers Bay starting line of the 1985 Junior Iditarod. Lance took first place in the race.*
(Bill Sherwonit)

hazard of Iditarod mushers. The drivers' main concern is the dogs. They are given the highest priority. Rest comes only after the dogs have been tended. Usually, the rest is not long enough — mushers often fall asleep while driving their teams. Some mushers tie themselves to their sleds. Many don't. It's not unheard of for mushers to fall off their sleds after falling asleep while the team is on the move.

*Three sled dogs watch the world go by while waiting for the start of the 1981 Iditarod race.* (Brad W. Ebel)

LEFT: *Musher Joee Redington Jr., who has finished in the top ten in the Fur Rendezvous World Championship and North American Championship sled dog races, drives his team around a bend along the trail of the 1984 world championship. Redington finished the race in eighth place.* (Jane Gnass)

BELOW: *Musher Libby Riddles drives her team across Norton Bay, toward the Koyuk checkpoint, during the 1985 Iditarod Trail Sled Dog Race.* (Bill Sherwonit)

# Father of the Iditarod

When Joe Redington Sr. talked in the early 1970s of a thousand-mile sled dog race across the state, he was labeled the "Don Quixote of Alaska." Yet in less than a dozen years, the Iditarod Trail Sled Dog Race grew from a never-will-happen fantasy into an international event.

And the man most responsible for making the impossible dream come true, Joe Redington Sr., earned worldwide acclaim for his efforts.

It's ironic, in a way. Outside of Alaska, Redington may be the best-known of the state's "modern" sled dog racers despite the fact that his name is not to be found on any list of Alaskan mushing champions. Redington has never won a major race. His best finish in the Iditarod is fifth. His approach to sled dog racing has always stressed having fun rather than winning titles.

Redington's fame came late in life. He was born February 1, 1917, "in a tent on the Chisolm Trail in Oklahoma." His father James was a farmer, rancher and oil-field worker, a drifting laborer. His mother was an "Oklahoma outlaw who took off for the hills" soon after Joe's birth.

James Redington and his two boys,

*Joe Redington Sr. relaxes at a checkpoint following a particularly harrowing stretch of trail during the 1984 Iditarod race.*
(*Anchorage Times*)

Joe and Ray, led a nomadic life, traveling throughout the country. Finally, in 1948, their travels brought them to Alaska.

Shortly after crossing the border the Redingtons stopped to gas up their Jeep. The owners of the service station presented them with a gift, a puppy.

"I wasn't in Alaska more than 10 minutes before I owned my first Alaskan husky," Joe says.

The Redingtons weren't rich, but Joe used what money he had to buy land in Knik. By chance, the land that he bought was adjacent to the Iditarod Trail. Joe's father also bought some land in Knik; the Iditarod Trail passed right through that property.

In fall 1948, Redington met Lee Ellexson, an Alaskan sourdough who had carried mail by dogsled along the Iditarod Trail in the early 1900s.

"Lee sold me on sled dogs," Redington says. "He had seven big old huskies. He'd tell me stories of the old days and took me out on the trail. Lee sold me on mushing."

By the end of his first winter in Alaska, Redington owned 40 dogs and had started up his Knik Kennels. At first, he used the dogs for work rather than recreation. They helped to haul equipment and the logs Redington used to build his cabins. They were also used on rescue and recovery missions. Redington, who had been an Army paratrooper during World War II, contracted out his services with the U.S. Air Force to recover the wreckage of aircraft that had crashed and to rescue or recover the remains of military personnel involved in the crashes. From 1949 until 1957, he used teams of 20 to 30 dogs to haul millions

Constance Seppala, widow of famed musher Leonhard Seppala, draws starting position 19 for Joe Redington Sr. in the first Iditarod race in February 1967. (Anchorage Times)

LEFT: Joe Redington Sr. harnesses his lead dog before the start of a recent Iditarod Trail Sled Dog Race. Redington and Dorothy Page were instrumental in organizing the race, first run on a 50-mile course in 1967 and expanded to its present 1,100 miles in 1973. (Ron Wendt)

BELOW: Joe Redington Sr. started his Knik Kennels shortly after coming to Alaska in 1948. He originally used the dogs for work — hauling wood and equipment, on search and rescue operations and in his business as a big-game guide. (J. Schultz)

of dollars worth of aircraft and hundreds of servicemen from remote mountainous areas. From 1954 to 1968, he also used dog teams in his work as a big-game guide.

But always, there was an interest in the Iditarod Trail.

In the early 1950s, Joe and his wife, Vi, began clearing portions of the trail and working to have it named part of the National Historic Trail System. (Congress finally designated the Iditarod a National Historic Trail in 1976.)

Then, in 1966, Redington joined Dorothy Page in organizing the Iditarod Trail Centennial Race. The sled dog gospel according to Joe has been spread far and wide. The Iditarod has grown into a true international event, each year including entrants from overseas.

## The Yukon Quest

Organizers of the Yukon Quest International Sled Dog Race never intended their race to compete head-to-head with the famous Iditarod. It's true that both races are about 1,000 miles, but that's where the similarity ends.

The Yukon Quest, started in 1984, was originally conceived as an economical alternative to the Iditarod. One of the early goals of the 1,000-mile race between Fairbanks and Whitehorse, Yukon Territory, was to attract mushers who wanted to test their skills and teams over a long and difficult course, but were unable to run in the Iditarod. So the race was kept as simple as possible.

Another major goal of the Yukon Quest

*A musher and his team finish the l985 Yukon Quest International Sled Dog Race. The race, between Fairbanks and Whitehorse, Yukon Territory, began in 1984 as an alternative for long-distance mushers.*
(Courtesy of the Fairbanks Convention and Visitors Bureau)

has been to strengthen the historical ties between Alaska and the Yukon. The race route retraces many of the trails used by early prospectors, freighters and mail carriers. The Klondike trail, between Whitehorse, Lake Laberge and Dawson; the Yukon River trail, connecting Dawson, Eagle and Circle City; and the Circle to Fairbanks trail form integral parts of the race.

Race rules and regulations were established to distinguish the Quest from the Iditarod. To even out the competition, teams were limited to a maximum of 12 dogs (the Iditarod allows 18) and a minimum of eight to start the race. All but one of the race checkpoints are located along roads, which allows mushers to keep expenses down by driving in, rather than flying in, their food.

While the Iditarod has 27 checkpoints scattered along its 1,100-mile route, the Quest has only seven, making distances between checkpoints much longer. The longest haul, between Dawson City and Carmacks, is nearly 300 miles. Food and other supplies for this stretch can add more than 300 pounds to the weight of the sled.

One other notable variation is that the Quest changes directions on alternating years, providing Fairbanks and Whitehorse with both starts and finishes.

The Quest, like the Iditarod, emphasizes dog care. In fact, Quest officials have especially stressed the importance of the dogs' well-being. One of the race rules

*Mary Shields runs her team along the Yukon Quest trail outside Fairbanks during the 1986 race to Whitehorse.* (Ron Lambert)

95

*Joe May of Trapper Creek stops along the trail to check his dogs' feet during the 1986 Yukon Quest race.* (Ron Lambert)

*Joe Runyon gets a winning hug after coming in first in the 1985 Yukon Quest sled dog race.* (Charles T. Whitaker)

included to ensure proper care allows mushers to drop a maximum of three dogs. This encourages mushers to take care of their teams and not push them too hard.

Although the Quest's purses and press coverage do not yet approach that of the Iditarod, the race has managed to survive its infancy in good shape to become the major long-distance mushing event in the Interior. In 1987, Bill Cotter of Nenana won a $15,000 prize for completing the course in 12 days, 4 hours and 34 minutes. Dave Monson of Manley, husband of Iditarod musher Susan Butcher, won the 1988 Yukon Quest in 12 days, 5 hours and 6 minutes.

# The North American Championship
*by Pete Bowers*

Following the decline of sled dog racing in the Nome area, brought about by both dwindling gold mining activities and World War I, the focus of competitive events turned to the Interior. Within a few years, Fairbanks took over as the "dog mushing capital of Alaska" and, since 1927, has hosted a series of major sled dog races.

Dog racing was interrupted in 1941 with the outbreak of World War II, and did not resume again until 1946, when the challenging North American Championship Sled Dog Derby was organized. Originally run as a four-day, 74-mile event, it settled in 1949 to approximately its present schedule of 3 days and 70 miles.

The North American Championship quickly re-established the levels of excitement that existed for dog racing prior to the war. The North American captured many of the elements of the earlier races, such as consecutive heats held on separate days, and emphasis on speed and endurance, but added its own unique stamp, the grueling "extra 10" tacked onto the third day of competition. The additional 10 miles of racing on the third day has taken its toll on many an undertrained or poorly prepared team and driver.

Today, the Open Class North American Championship in Fairbanks annually draws the top sprint race drivers from Alaska, Canada and the lower 48. The 1986 purse was $25,000, with first place taking home $5,600.

The earliest of the postwar North

*Horace "Holy" Smoke, 1951, 1952 and 1953 winner of the Fairbanks North American Championship, poses with some of his trophies. It is said Smoke owed much of his success to his 48-pound lead dog, Canyon. With her in the lead, Smoke finished the 1953 race more than 7 minutes ahead of the nearest competitor. Canyon died in the year following the 1953 race and Smoke was never able to regain the championship.*
(Everett Wilde, Alaska Dog Mushers Association Collection)

American race courses followed trails along the Chena and Tanana rivers, but were changed in 1953 to the Creamer's Field area. One leg of these courses included parts of what are now the University of Alaska Ski Trail, and also extended into Goldstream Valley along Sheep Creek Road. In recent years, the start and finish line has been on Second Avenue in downtown Fairbanks.

Through the years, a number of familiar names have come to be associated with the North American Championship. The first two races were won by Andy Kokrine. The 1950 winner, Gareth Wright, showed his perseverance and competitiveness by winning his second North American crown in 1983. In 1953, Air Force Lt. Col. Norman Vaughan flew a dog team owned by Keith Bryar from the East Coast to Fairbanks to compete in the races.

From 1951 through 1953, the competition was dominated by Horace "Holy"

**TOP:** *Despite an injured front foot, Venus led Gareth Wright's team to a courageous victory in the 1950 North American Championship Sled Dog Race. Although the foot remained swollen for some time, Venus continued to run lead for Wright through 1954.* (Robinson Studios, courtesy of Earl Norris)

**LEFT:** *Jeff Studdert (center, in fur hat) officiates at the weight-pull contest during a 1950s Fairbanks Ice Carnival. Studdert was known as the "grand old man" of the Fairbanks racing scene.* (Alaska Dog Mushers Association Collection)

*George Attla, the "Huslia Hustler," takes off down Second Avenue in Fairbanks at the start of the 1980 North American Championship.* (Pete Bowers)

Smoke of Stevens Village. At the time, he became only the third musher, in addition to Bob Buzby and Johnny Allen, to win one of the major Fairbanks races three consecutive years. It is said that Smoke owed much of his success to his 48-pound female leader named Canyon, one of the great lead dogs of all time. With her in the lead, Smoke finished the 1953, 70-mile race more than seven minutes ahead of his

nearest competitor. Canyon died in the year following the 1953 race, and "Holy" Smoke was never able to regain the championship.

The 1950s and 1960s saw the development of sled dog racing in Fairbanks with a greater-than-ever emphasis on scientific feeding, breeding and training, which today are virtually mandatory elements for success. One of the major contributors to this increased awareness is former North American Champion Dr. Roland Lombard of Wayland, Massachusetts. Lombard, who began his racing career in 1929 with a team of dogs which included two of Seppala's Siberians, won his first North American race in 1959. Lombard came to

be a favorite among the fiercely loyal Fairbanks crowds.

"Doc" Lombard's record six North American wins remained unequaled until George Attla tied him in 1979. The Lombard-Attla duels of the 1960s and 1970s have become legendary. In 1986, Attla broke the tie and became the winningest musher of all time, when he recorded his seventh North American win. (For good measure, Attla added his eighth win in 1987.) In 1988, Marvin Kokrine of North Pole drove the fastest team, edging out second-place finisher George Attla by just 15 seconds to complete the race in a total elapsed time of 225 minutes, 49 seconds.

*As husband Gareth looks on, Vera Wright prepares to start in the Women's North American Championship Race in Fairbanks in the mid-1950s.*
(Courtesy of Earl Norris)

That win was especially sweet for Attla, since the previous year's winner, a young Canadian musher named Eddie Streeper, had pronounced the 53-year-old Attla "washed up."

The Women's North American race was run in Fairbanks between 1952 and 1982, when it made way for the Mini North American. Past champions include six-time winner Jean Bryar, four-time winner Rosie Losonsky and three-time winners Effie Kokrine and Roxy Wright. Other perennial favorites of years past include Libby Wescott, Natalie Norris, and Kit MacInnes.

# Mushers Hall of Fame

The Mushers Hall of Fame was established in 1967, by members of the Wasilla-Knik Centennial Committee and the Iditarod Trail Committee, to "salute the special breed of Alaskans and others who have gained fame in mushing circles."

Leonhard Seppala, a legend because of his exploits in the All Alaska Sweepstakes and diphtheria serum run of 1925, was the first musher elected to the hall. Nine other sled dog racers and several non-racing contributors to mushing were also named in 1967.

The hall is housed in the Knik Museum, at about Mile 13 of Knik Road. The Wasilla-Knik-Willow Creek Historical Society serves as caretaker of the museum.

A brief description of each member follows. An asterisk indicates a charter member.

*Alexander A. "Scotty" Allan: Three-time winner of the All Alaska Sweepstakes, he was considered one of the premier mushers

*Johnny Allen takes off from the starting line, under the Cushman Street Bridge, in the 1937 Ice Carnival Race in Fairbanks.*
(University of Alaska Archives, Fairbanks)

in Nome in the early 1900s. He also helped to train several hundred sled dogs for use in the mountains of France during World War I.

**Johnny Allen:** Indian musher from the lower Yukon River known for both his racing and breeding talents. He developed his own special line of dogs by interbreeding Irish setters, Alaskan huskies and wolves.

**George Attla:** Most famous of the "Huslia Hustlers," Attla overcame a boyhood bout with tuberculosis to become Alaska's winningest musher. He is also renowned for his dog-training talents.

**Percy Blatchford:** Second in All Alaska Sweepstakes in 1909 and third in 1908. More famous for his "dependable mail runs than for winning races," according to Carrie McLain.

**\*Faye Delzene:** Another of Nome's well-known dog-drivers of the early 1900s. He won the 1913 sweepstakes race and placed second to Seppala in 1916.

**Ben Downing:** Laid out the first sled dog mail trails from Dawson, Yukon Territory, to Alaska, and was noted for his dependable mail delivery in even the harshest conditions.

**\*John Hegness:** First winner of the All Alaska Sweepstakes.

**\*John "Iron Man" Johnson:** Iron Man was

*George Attla, despite a career-long knee problem, has become known as Alaska's winningest musher. As of 1986, Attla had captured 17 championship titles. Here, Attla stands behind his team during the 1983 World Championship Sled Dog Race.*
(Brad W. Ebel)

a two-time winner of the All Alaska Sweepstakes. He also set the all-time sweepstakes record in 1910 by finishing the 408-mile race in 74 hours, 14 minutes and 37 seconds.

**Andy Kokrine:** Noted native musher who raced dogs in the Interior from the mid-1940s through the mid-1950s, Kokrine won the inaugural North America Championship Sled Dog Race following the end of World War II.

**Dr. Roland Lombard:** A veterinarian from Wayland, Massachusetts, and the most successful Outsider ever to compete in Alaska dog racing. Perhaps most important, however, were his contributions to improved dog-care practices.

**Col. Marvin "Muktuk" Marston:** Traveled hundreds of miles by dog team during the late 1930s while organizing the Alaska Territorial Guard. He was also a major financial contributor to the inaugural Iditarod Trail Sled Dog Race in 1973.

**\*Carrie McLain:** Pioneer Nome resident who knew many of the early mushers in that gold-boom town of the early 1900s.

**\*Gen. William "Billy" Mitchell:** The "Father of the U.S. Air Force" was an enthusiastic sled dog racing fan. He became sold on sled dogs while using them for work connected with building a telegraph line across Alaska.

**Earl and Natalie Norris:** Earl was the founding father of the Fur Rendezvous Sled Dog Race and helped to revive sled dog racing in Alaska during the late 1940s. Both he and Natalie raised and drove championship teams in Rondy races, and

**ABOVE:** *Dr. Roland Lombard poses with his leaders, Chuck and Scamp, following their 1959 victory in the North American Championship Sled Dog Race in Fairbanks. Lombard, a veterinarian from Wayland, Massachusetts, is well known as the most successful non-Alaskan musher to compete here.* (Jim Couch; reprinted from *ALASKA SPORTSMAN®*)

**RIGHT:** *Earl and Natalie Norris, shown here at their kennel, breed, raise, train and race Siberian huskies.* (Bill Sherwonit)

were founding members of the Alaska Sled Dog and Racing Association.

**Dorothy Page:** The first Iditarod Trail Race was staged in 1967 largely through her efforts. Although the two-day, 50-mile Seppala Memorial Race followed only nine miles of the Iditarod Trail, it paved the way for the eventual 1,100-mile race from Anchorage to Nome.

**\*Raymond Paul:** First three-time winner

*Known as "Mother of the Iditarod," Dorothy Page was instrumental in organizing the first Iditarod sled dog race in 1967.* (J. Schultz)

*Joe and Vi Redington pose in Nome following the 1982 Iditarod race. The two have devoted years to promoting the race.* (J. Schultz)

of the Anchorage Fur Rendezvous. A Native from Galena, Paul drowned in a boating accident in 1956.

**\*Fox Maule Ramsay:** Sled dog owner and driver who helped to introduce Siberian huskies to Alaska.

**Joe and Vi Redington:** Joe and his wife,

Vi, spent years in their effort to have the Iditarod Trail added to the National Historic Trail System and in promoting the Iditarod Trail Sled Dog Race. Both also raced sled dogs.

**\*Dr. Joseph Herman Romig:** Subject of Eva Greenslit Anderson's *Dog Team Doctor* (1941), Romig used dog teams around Bethel to visit patients in isolated areas.

**\*Emil St. Godard:** Godard, from Le Pas, Manitoba, was well-known in Canadian and New England mushing circles. His most famous victory was over Seppala in the sled dog demonstration race at the 1932 Winter Olympics in Lake Placid, N.Y.

**\*Eva B. "Short" Seeley:** Along with her husband, Milton, Eva Seeley of New Hampshire raised and trained dogs used by the Byrd Antarctic Expedition in the late 1920s. She also trained sled dogs for U.S. Army, Navy and Air Force expeditions and was chief advisor for "Operation Deepfreeze" in the Antarctic in 1955. She was the only woman to compete in the 1932 Olympics demonstration race.

**\*Leonhard Seppala:** Three-time winner of the All Alaska Sweepstakes in 1915, 1916 and 1917, Seppala is best known for his crucial role in the diphtheria serum run to Nome in 1925. He also popularized the use of Siberian huskies in sled dog racing.

**\*Raymond L. Thompson:** Long-time promoter of mushing. For many years he used sled dogs while working traplines. He is also former publisher of *Northern Dog News* and *Siberian Husky News*.

**\*Judge James Wickersham:** An Alaskan judge and later delegate to the U.S. Congress from Alaska, Wickersham used

*Dr. Joseph Herman Romig (in fur hat and parka), known as the "dog team doctor," poses with his Anchorage hospital staff during a staff picnic in February, 1934. The group dressed up in Indian costumes for the occasion.* (The Anchorage Museum)

dog teams in connection with his court work. His book *Old Yukon: Tales, Trails and Trials* (1938) records some of his sled dog experiences.

*Slim Williams: Traveled 5,600 miles by dog team in 1932 and 1933 to publicize the need for a highway from Alaska to the Lower 48 and to promote Alaska at the Century of Progress World's Fair in Chicago.

*Slim Williams, posing with his lead dog, Rembrandt, reached national acclaim when he made a 5,600-mile dogsled trek from 1932 to 1933 from Copper Center to Chicago to promote Alaska at the Century of Progress World's Fair.* (Jack B. Updyke)

# Raising Sled Dogs

## Breeding Racing Dogs

In the beginning, there were malamutes, big, strong dogs built and bred for working. Malamutes and other large sled dogs, such as the Mackenzie River huskies, were fine for hauling freight, running traplines or delivering mail, but they weren't especially well-adapted to sled dog racing. They didn't have enough stamina or long-distance speed.

Then came the Siberians, straight from Russia. When introduced to Nome during the All Alaska Sweepstakes series, Siberian huskies turned out to be excellent racing dogs. Much smaller than the working dogs, they proved to be faster and had more endurance. Their only fault was that they were often difficult to handle.

Finally came the mixed breeds, the mutts. Huskies were bred with other dogs — hounds, setters, Salukis, spaniels, German shepherds and even wolves. And these mutts, the husky-hound mixes, took over the show. They soon became the best sled dogs.

*Leonhard Seppala's team of Siberian huskies rests in the snow. Although they are beautiful dogs, most mushers consider purebred Siberians not competitive enough for racing.* (Alaska Northwest Publishing)

Alaskan huskies are such mixed-breed dogs. Some mushers won't even attempt to define what an Alaskan husky is. But the usual definition given is "a northern breed of dog with a heavy, double coat, curly tail and pointed ears. Husky looking, yet with definite hound blood in them."

According to musher Charlie Champaine, "All the top teams are made of mixed breeds. There are no winning teams with Siberians or other purebreds. They just aren't competitive."

Earl Norris is one of the few mushers to continue raising purebred, registered Siberians. He disagrees with the notion that they don't match up to the mutts, saying "Siberians are better than most people give them credit for. . . . They're more independent. . . . Siberians can be just as fast if you get the good ones."

Yet most mushers seem to agree that purebred huskies all too often have disposition problems. And, says Champaine, they often have poor feet that are too easily injured or cut up.

Hounds, meanwhile, can contribute genes for strong, tough feet and good racing attitudes.

Gareth Wright has one of the more famous mixed-breed lines. Wright began his Aurora husky line by mixing Irish setter, wolf and husky in an attempt to copy the dogs bred in the 1930s by famous native musher Johnny Allen.

LEFT: *A litter of pups belonging to Charlie Champaine curls up in front of their dog house.* (Bill Sherwonit)

ABOVE: *Breeding programs are designed to produce dogs with only the best physical and mental qualities. This husky shows great determination as she pulls a sled across an extremely slick stretch of ice.* (Stuart Pechek)

107

The major strengths of Wright's line are exceptionally tough feet, great endurance, a phenomenal desire to work and a minimal amount of training needed to get into shape. On the other hand, Wright admits they tend to be one-man dogs that don't take well to strangers, do not fare well in warm temperatures, can be hyper and/or sulky and may quit when pushed too hard. So it goes. Every line has its assets and debits.

Another well-known line of dogs was developed by George Attla, who continued and improved upon the line of dogs from Huslia and the Koyukuk River region.

Breeding programs play an important role in improving the overall quality of dogs. The ultimate goal of such programs is to eliminate non-productive traits while keeping those qualities considered desirable in racing dogs.

There are two methods of breeding: inbreeding and out-crossing, or out-breeding. Inbreeding involves dogs that are closely related, such as mother-son, father-daughter or sister-brother. It results in stronger characteristics, good and bad. In outbreeding, dogs that are not closely related are bred. It's a slower, less drastic way of achieving desired qualities.

*Gareth Wright drives his mixed-breed team in the 1985 World Championship race in Anchorage. Wright is well-known for his Aurora husky line of dogs, bred by crossing Irish setter, wolf and husky.* (Jane Gnass)

The goal of all breeding programs is to produce fast dogs, with tough feet, good conformation, proper size, great endurance and good dispositions; that is, a willingness to please and a strong desire to run. Only rarely are dogs produced that combine all those elements. But there is always hope.

And although experimentation continues in the search for the perfect sled dog, many

*Two alert sled dogs watch with interest as mushers prepare their teams for a race.* (J. Schultz)

mushers use a simple guideline: breed the best to the best. Members of a championship team — particularly male leaders — are sure to be in demand for outbreeding purposes.

# Feeding Sled Dogs

With an increased awareness of and commitment to the well-being of dogs, there have been notable improvements in dog care and feeding.

"Dogs are creatures of routine," says musher Charlie Champaine, who runs a feed business and supplies dog food to many of the sled dog racers in the state.

"The smart mushers feed their dogs consistently year-round. They don't feed one thing in the summer and another before races. Consistency and quality is the key."

Champaine feeds his dogs basically the same diet year-round, giving them chicken, beef, liver, eggs, wheat-germ oil, corn oil, some commercial feed and liquid vitamins.

Improvements in diet also have been made in the realm of long-distance racing, particularly the Iditarod. The first year of the race, most mushers used commercial feed and/or fish. One exception was Dick Wilmarth.

According to Joe Redington Sr., Wilmarth began the race feeding his

*Most long-distance mushers rely on a meat-rich diet to maintain their dogs' strength along the trail. Iditarod mushers carry a variety of food for their teams, such as horsemeat, beef, liver, chicken fat, lamb, whitefish and commercial food.* (J. Schultz)

dogs salmon. At Rainy Pass, he obtained some beaver and started feeding it to the dogs. Not coincidently, perhaps, Wilmarth won the race.

Gradually, more and more Iditarod mushers began to rely on meat-rich diets. Redington, like Champaine, feeds his dogs such a diet year-round. He comments, "One thing that hurts a lot of mushers is that they change their [dogs'] diets right before a race. Then the dogs end up with a case of diarrhea. To lower expenses, people cut down on the quality of their food. They may not know it, but they're also cutting the strength of their dogs."

Redington feeds his dogs once a day.

*Along the Iditarod Trail, Libby Riddles feeds her dogs at the White Mountain checkpoint. On long-distance races, it is important to have dogs that eat willingly.* (Bill Sherwonit)

*Bill Yankee stops during the 1982 Iditarod Trail Sled Dog Race at the Finger Lake checkpoint to cook a pot of food for his dogs.* (J. Schultz)

During the off-season, each dog is fed about a quarter-pound of food; during training, the intake is upped to a half-pound per meal and during races, the size of the meal can increase to several pounds, depending on weather and race conditions. Occasionally, Redington will skip a day of feeding if it looks like the dogs are getting fat. But on the Iditarod, "You want 'em a little heavier," he says. "There's a balance; you don't want 'em too fat or too thin."

Redington also stresses the importance of water in the dogs' diet. "I keep the dogs' water dishes filled all the time," he says. "I give them as much as they want." In races, Redington and many other mushers add flavoring to the water, to make it more attractive to the dogs.

Redington's dogs' diet in summer consists of lamb, liver, commercial food and bulk, "to soak up a lot of water." In the fall, he'll add beef and whitefish. A few weeks before races, he will also begin adding eggs. And, during the race, the dogs are treated to beaver snacks.

"Beaver is real popular," he says. "It's easy to digest, the dogs love it and it has a tremendous amount of energy with staying power. I feed each dog one or two pounds of beaver at each checkpoint."

Another treat that many Iditarod mushers feed their dogs is honeyballs.

"I feed honeyballs as a snack between checkpoints," Redington says. "They're about the size of a baseball, weigh about a pound and are real high in

*Some mushers feed honeyballs to their dogs along the trail. These snacks, made of lean beef, honey, oil, yeast, vitamins, bonemeal, eggs and electrolytes, are high in calories and easily digested.* (J. Schultz)

calories and easily digested. They're real good for keeping oil in the dog's hair. That especially helps the feet. It helps prevent ice from balling up, which can cut up a dog's feet. . . . "

The recipe for Redington's honeyballs: mix 250 pounds of lean beef (4 percent fat); 60 pounds of Montana honey; five gallons of safflower oil; one gallon of wheat germ oil; 10 pounds of brewer's yeast; 20 pounds of multivitamins; 10 pounds of bonemeal; four No. 10 cans of powdered eggs; and an electrolyte to provide salt.

The dogs love it, Redington says. And best of all, it's good for them.

## Training Sled Dogs

Sled dogs begin their apprenticeships early in life. The age of first hook-up varies from kennel to kennel and musher to musher. More important than the age of the dogs, however, is their treatment. The golden rules of pup training admonish handlers to go easy, go slow, keep things light and make it fun. Mushers also agree that it is important to handle and play with pups so that they become accustomed to humans.

Commonly, dogs are taken on training walks or runs before ever being put in harness. Such outings help the pups become familiar with the different types of terrain and weather conditions they will later meet on the trail.

First harnessing is done cautiously, usually at four or five months of age. If the experience isn't fun, the end product will be a scared dog, a dog that will not enjoy running in front of a sled. A principal goal of the early training runs is to acquaint the pups with running in harness, to teach them to run as a unit. Most mushers run pups in teams with more experienced dogs.

Evaluation of the pups begins immediately, with the mushers separating the

*Musher Susan Butcher uses a dog walker (top) and three-wheeler to train her dogs. Butcher starts working with her pups at an early age, taking them on training hikes before harnessing them for the first time at four or five months.* (Both by J. Schultz)

*Susan Butcher leads a group of pups on a training run at Joe Redington Sr.'s Knik Kennels. Butcher likes to make a dog's early training an enjoyable experience.*
(Alissa Crandall)

haves from the have-nots. Charlie Champaine has a four-tier system of classification: for-sures, good possibilities, maybe-with-some-lucks and not-a-prayers.

In their search for the born leaders, most drivers will test out each dog in the lead

*The cost of keeping sled dogs in top condition for racing is high — food, veterinary care and equipment for a team can amount to thousands of dollars a year. Sponsors help pay a musher's expenses in return for advertising or publicity. General Foods is one of Joe Redington Sr.'s sponsors; Redington has made television commercials for Tang, one of the company's products.* (J. Schultz)

position at an early age, to see whether he has what it takes. The ideal leader is fast, intelligent, hard-working, responsible, mentally tough, honest and eager to please. Because a musher rides (or runs) behind the team, he must rely on the leader to obey commands immediately. (In fact, some mushers say that prime leaders can at times sense a musher's desires before they are even spoken.) Dogs with all those qualities are rare.

No longer do mushers wait for the snow to fly before hitching up sled dog teams for the start of their annual training runs. Dogs can be harnessed and hitched up to three- and four-wheel training carts in September or even earlier. And, some long-distance mushers train their teams year-round.

Whatever the starting date, the basic philosophy is the same. Begin with short, slow runs and gradually build up the length of the runs and accompanying demands on

*Pete Shepherd figured the best way to get acquainted with his new lead dog was to take her along with him during a spring muskrat hunt. Originally owned by Andy Jimmy of Minto Village, Peggy is shown here sometime in the mid-1960s, hitched up to a sled full of trapping gear. By the time the hunt was over, Peggy and her new master were good friends.* (Pete Shepherd)

the dogs. To ensure control, mushers usually begin with small teams.

When the training has finally been completed, the sprint dogs will have run several hundred to more than a thousand miles. Long-distance dogs will have traveled even farther, from 1,500 to more than 3,000 miles, depending on the musher.

And if the training has been done correctly, the musher finds himself in command of a finely tuned machine that is ready and willing to run.

**LEFT:** *Branded as a puppy a "no-chance" sled dog by owner Joe Redington Sr., Feets later proved himself to be a hard-working leader, running five Iditarod races for Redington. Feets is one of only a few dogs to be elected to the Mushers Hall of Fame.* (J. Schultz)

**BELOW:** *In harness for the first time, Athena and Pumpkin, owned by musher Susan Will of Fairbanks, seem to be wondering what to do next.* (Pete Bowers)

*Musher Rick Mackey poses with his lead dogs Jody (left) and Preacher. The ideal lead dog possesses speed, intelligence, honesty and a willingness to please.* (J. Schultz)

BELOW: *Charlie Champaine's team keeps to the trail, apparently unaware that their musher has been dumped off the sled.* (Third Eye Photography)

RIGHT: *Alladin, a descendent of Leonhard Seppala's Togo, runs at the lead of Earl Norris' team. Alladin was the mainstay of Norris' teams during the late 1940s and early 1950s.* (Courtesy of Earl Norris)

RIGHT: *Pups at Joe Redington Sr.'s Knik Kennels romp over a fallen log. Redington does not put his dogs into harness until they are 1 year old.* (J. Schultz)

# Alaska Geographic Back Issues

**The North Slope, Vol. 1, No. 1.** Charter issue. *Out of print.*

**One Man's Wilderness, Vol. 1, No. 2.** *Out of print.* (Book edition available, $19.95.)

**Admiralty . . . Island in Contention, Vol. 1, No. 3.** In-depth review of Southeast's Admiralty Island. 78 pages, $5.

**Fisheries of the North Pacific: History, Species, Gear & Processes, Vol. 1, No. 4.** *Out of print.* (Book edition available, $24.95.)

**The Alaska-Yukon Wild Flowers Guide, Vol. 2, No. 1.** *Out of print.* (Book edition available, $12.95.)

**Richard Harrington's Yukon, Vol. 2, No. 2.** *Out of print.*

**Prince William Sound, Vol. 2, No. 3.** *Out of print.*

**Yakutat: The Turbulent Crescent, Vol. 2, No. 4.** *Out of print.*

**Glacier Bay: Old Ice, New Land, Vol. 3, No. 1.** *Out of print.*

**The Land: Eye of the Storm, Vol. 3, No. 2.** *Out of print.*

**Richard Harrington's Antarctic, Vol. 3, No. 3.** Reviews Antarctica and islands of southern polar regions, territories of mystery and controversy. Fold-out map. 104 pages, $8.95.

**The Silver Years of the Alaska Canned Salmon Industry: An Album of Historical Photos, Vol. 3, No. 4.** *Out of print.*

**Alaska's Volcanoes: Northern Link in the Ring of Fire, Vol. 4, No. 1.** *Out of print.*

**The Brooks Range: Environmental Watershed, Vol. 4, No. 2.** *Out of print.*

**Kodiak: Island of Change, Vol. 4, No. 3.** *Out of print.*

**Wilderness Proposals: Which Way for Alaska's Lands?, Vol. 4, No. 4.** *Out of print.*

**Cook Inlet Country, Vol. 5, No. 1.** *Out of print.*

**Southeast: Alaska's Panhandle, Vol. 5, No. 2.** Explores southeastern Alaska's maze of fjords and islands, forests and mountains, from Dixon Entrance to Icy Bay, including all of the Inside Passage. The book profiles every town, and reviews the region's history, economy, people, attractions and future. Fold-out map. 192 pages, $12.95.

**Bristol Bay Basin, Vol. 5, No. 3.** *Out of print.*

**Alaska Whales and Whaling, Vol. 5, No. 4.** The wonders of whales in Alaska — their life cycles, travels and travails — are examined, with an authoritative history of commercial and subsistence whaling in the North. Includes a fold-out poster of 14 major whale species in Alaska in perspective, color photos and illustrations, with historical photos and line drawings. 144 pages, $19.95.

**Yukon-Kuskokwim Delta, Vol. 6, No. 1.** *Out of print.*

**The Aurora Borealis, Vol. 6, No. 2.** Explores the northern lights in history and today; their cause, how they work, and their importance in contemporary science. 96 pages, $7.95.

**Alaska's Native People, Vol. 6, No. 3.** Examines the worlds of the Inupiat and Yupik Eskimo, Athabascan, Aleut, Tlingit, Haida and Tsimshian. Fold-out map of Native villages and language areas. 304 pages, $24.95.

**The Stikine River, Vol. 6, No. 4.** River route to three Canadian gold strikes, the Stikine is the largest and most navigable of several rivers that flow from northwestern Canada through southeastern Alaska to the Pacific Ocean. Fold-out map. 96 pages, $9.95.

**Alaska's Great Interior, Vol. 7, No. 1.** Examines the people, communites, economy, and wilderness of Alaska's rich Interior, the immense valley between the Alaska Range and Brooks Range. Fold-out map. 128 pages, $9.95.

**A Photographic Geography of Alaska, Vol. 7, No. 2.** A visual tour through the six regions of Alaska: Southeast, Southcentral/Gulf Coast, Alaska Peninsula and Aleutians, Bering Sea Coast, Arctic and Interior. 192 pages, $15.95.

**The Aleutians, Vol. 7, No. 3.** Home of the Aleut, a tremendous wildlife spectacle, a major World War II battleground, and an important arm of Alaska's commercial fishing industry. Fold-out map. 224 pages, $14.95.

**Klondike Lost: A Decade of Photographs by Kinsey & Kinsey, Vol. 7, No. 4.** *Out of print.* (Book edition available, $12.95.)

**Wrangell-Saint Elias, Vol. 8, No. 1.** Alaska's only designated World Heritage Area, this mountain wilderness takes in the nation's largest national park in its sweep from the Copper River across the Wrangell Mountains to the southern tip of the Saint Elias Range near Yakutat. Fold-out map. 144 pages, $19.95.

**Alaska Mammals, Vol. 8, No. 2.** Reviews in anecdotes and facts the entire spectrum of Alaska's wildlife. 184 pages, $12.95.

**The Kotzebue Basin, Vol. 8, No. 3.** Examines northwestern Alaska's thriving trading area of Kotzebue Sound and the Kobuk and Noatak river basins. 184 pages, $12.95.

**Alaska National Interest Lands, Vol. 8, No. 4.** Reviews each of Alaska's national interest land (d-2 lands) selections, outlining location, size, access and briefly describes special attractions. 242 pages, $14.95.

**Alaska's Glaciers, Vol. 9, No. 1.** Examines in-depth the massive rivers of ice, their composition, exploration, present-day distribution and scientific significance. Illustrated with many contemporary color and historical black-and-white photos, the text includes separate discussions of more than a dozen glacial regions. 144 pages, $19.95

**Sitka and Its Ocean/Island World, Vol. 9, No. 2.** From the elegant capital of Russian America to a beautiful but modern port, Sitka, on Baranof Island, has become a commercial and cultural center for Southeastern Alaska. 128 pages, $19.95.

**Islands of the Seals: The Pribilofs, Vol. 9, No. 3.** Great herds of northern fur seals and immense flocks of seabirds share their island homeland with Aleuts brought to this remote Bering Sea outpost by Russians. 128 pages, $9.95.

**Alaska's Oil/Gas & Minerals Industry, Vol. 9, No. 4.** Experts detail the geological processes and resulting mineral and fossil fuel resources that contribute substantially to Alaska's economy. 216 pages, $12.95.

**Adventure Roads North: The Story of the Alaska Highway and Other Roads in *The MILEPOST*, Vol. 10, No. 1.** Reviews the history of Alaska's roads and takes a mile-by-mile look at the country they cross. 224 pages, $14.95.

**Anchorage and the Cook Inlet Basin, Vol. 10, No. 2.** Reviews in depth the commercial and urban center of the Last Frontier. Three fold-out maps. 168 pages, $14.95.

**Alaska's Salmon Fisheries, Vol. 10, No. 3.** A comprehensive look at Alaska's most valuable commercial fishery. 128 pages, $12.95.

**Up the Koyukuk, Vol. 10, No. 4.** Highlights the wildlife and traditional native lifestyle of this remote region of northcentral Alaska. 152 pages, $14.95.

**Nome: City of the Golden Beaches, Vol. 11, No. 1.** Reviews the colorful history of one of Alaska's most famous gold rush towns. 184 pages, $14.95.

**Alaska's Farms and Gardens, Vol. 11, No. 2.** An overview of the past, present and future of agriculture in Alaska, with details on growing your own vegetables in the North. 144 pages, $12.95.

**Chilkat River Valley, Vol. 11, No. 3.** Explores the mountain-rimmed valley at the head of the Inside Passage, its natural resources, and the residents who have settled there. 112 pages, $12.95.

**Alaska Steam, Vol. 11, No. 4.** Pictorial history of the pioneering Alaska Steamship Company. 160 pages, $12.95.

**Northwest Territories, Vol. 12, No. 1.** In-depth look at the magnificent wilderness of Canada's high Arctic. Fold-out map. 136 pages, $12.95.

**Alaska's Forest Resources, Vol. 12, No. 2.** Examines the botanical, recreational and economic value of Alaska's forests. 200 pages, $14.95.

**Alaska Native Arts and Crafts, Vol. 12, No. 3.** In-depth review of the art and artifacts of Alaska's Natives. 215 pages, $17.95.

**Our Arctic Year, Vol. 12, No. 4.** Compelling story of a year in the wilds of the Brooks Range. 150 pages, $12.95.

**Where Mountains Meet the Sea: Alaska's Gulf Coast, Vol. 13, No. 1.** Alaskan's first-hand descriptions of the 850-mile arc that crowns the Pacific Ocean from Kodiak to Cape Spencer at the entrance to southeastern Alaska's Inside Passage. 191 pages, $14.95.

**Backcountry Alaska, Vol. 13, No. 2.** A full-color look at the remote communities of Alaska. Companion volume to *The ALASKA WILDERNESS MILEPOST®.* 224 pages, $14.95.

**British Columbia's Coast/The Canadian Inside Passage, Vol. 13, No. 3.** Reviews the B.C. coast west of the Coast Mountain divide from mighty Vancouver and elegant Victoria in the south to the forested wilderness to the north, including the Queen Charlotte Islands. Fold-out map. 200 pages, $14.95.

**Lake Clark/Lake Iliamna Country, Vol. 13, No. 4.** Chronicles the human and natural history of the region that many claim has a sampling of all the best that Alaska has to offer in natural beauty. 152 pages, $14.95.

**Dogs of the North, Vol. 14, No. 1.** The first men to cross the Bering Land Bridge probably brought dogs to Alaska. This issue examines the development of northern breeds from the powerful husky and malemute to the fearless little Tahltan bear dog, the evolution of the dogsled, uses of dogs, and the history of sled-dog racing from the All-Alaska Sweepstakes of 1908 to the nationally televised Iditarod of today. 120 pages, $16.95.

**South/Southeast Alaska, Vol. 14, No. 2.** Reviews the natural and human resources of the southernmost tip of Alaska's Panhandle, from Sumner Strait to the Canadian border. Fold-out map. 120 pages, $14.95.

**Alaska's Seward Peninsula, Vol. 14, No. 3.** The Seward Peninsula is today's remnant of the Bering Land Bridge, gateway to an ancient America. This issue chronicles the blending of traditional Eskimo culture with the white man's persistent search for gold. Fold-out map. 112 pages, $14.95.

**The Upper Yukon Basin, Vol. 14, No. 4.** Yukoner Monty Alford describes this remote region, headwaters for one of the continent's mightiest rivers and gateway for some of Alaska's earliest pioneers. 117 pages, $14.95.

**Glacier Bay: Icy Wilderness, Vol. 15, No. 1.** Covers the 5,000-square-mile wilderness now known as Glacier Bay National Park and Preserve, including the natural and human history of the Glacier Bay area, its wildlife, how to get there, what to expect, and what changes now seem predictable. 103 pages, $14.95.

**Dawson City, Vol. 15, No. 2.** For two years just before the turn of the century, writes author Mike Doogan, news from Dawson City blazed like a nova around the world and a million people wanted to go there. Like a nova, the gold-rush burned out quickly, but its light still illuminates the city it built. In this issue Doogan examines the geology and the history of the Klondike, and why a million tourists want to go to Dawson while other gold-rush towns of the North are only collapsed cabins and faded memories. 94 pages, historic and contemporary photos, index, $14.95.

**Denali, Vol. 13, No. 3.** It was *Denali* to the Tanana Indians, *Doleika* to the nearby Tanainas, *Bolshaya Gora* to the Russians, all connoting size and height and scenic grandeur. A gold-prospector called it *McKinley* less than a century ago, and unfortunately that name endured. But the mountain massif in southcentral Alaska, by whatever name, has fascinated man from the primitive to the present. This book is an indepth guide to the Great One, its lofty neighbors and the surrounding wilderness now known as Denali National Park and Preserve. 94 pages, historic and contemporary photos, index $14.95.

**NEXT ISSUE:**
**Katmai, Vol. 16, No. 1.** This issue reviews the volcanic world of Katmai National Park and Preserve and adjoining Becharof National Wildlife Refuge. Home to some of the state's highest brown bear populations, this wilderness at the head of the Alaska Peninsula claims the Valley of 10,000 Smokes and its famous volcanoes. The natural and cultural history of one of Alaska's most turbulent landscapes comes to life in **Katmai.** To members in March 1989. Prices to be announced.

**ALL PRICES SUBJECT TO CHANGE.**

Your $30 membership in The Alaska Geographic Society includes four subsequent issues of *ALASKA GEOGRAPHIC®,* the Society's official quarterly. Please add $4 for non-U.S. membership.

Additional membership information is available upon request. Single copies of the *ALASKA GEOGRAPHIC®* back issues are also available. When ordering, please make payments in U.S. funds and add $1.50 postage/handling per copy. To order back issues send your check or money order and volumes desired to:

*The Alaska Geographic Society*

P.O. Box 93370, Anchorage, Alaska 99509